The
Art & Science
of Face Reading

"Jennifer Lamonica reveals the special messages of facial morphology that allow clinicians to better understand the stated and hidden needs of the patient before them. She brings to life the teachings of Dr. Gerald Epstein. I took his facial morphology class and am able to use what I learned to more easily ascertain a patient's inner dynamics and the way these dynamics may intersect with their health. As an adolescent and young adult medicine specialist, I know this special text brings the gift of understanding to the next generation of healers."

DORIS PASTORE, M.D., PROFESSOR OF PEDIATRICS
AT THE ICAHN SCHOOL OF MEDICINE,
MOUNT SINAI HOSPITAL, NEW YORK CITY

"In the field of holistic practice, harmony among the body-mind-spirit is the key to health and wellness. Identification of individual constitution, temperament, and other characteristics is important for the establishment of a therapeutic strategy. *The Art and Science of Face Reading* is invaluable to practitioners. It is illustrated, practical, and informative."

YEMENG CHEN, PH.D., L.AC., PRESIDENT OF
NEW YORK COLLEGE OF TRADITIONAL CHINESE MEDICINE

"Finally, a comprehensive book on face morphology! Nearly anyone can start reading faces quickly, accurately, and compassionately with the profound system of face reading based on this ancient and sacred art. Jennifer Lamonica shares powerful secrets gathered over her decades as an extraordinary chiropractor, acupuncturist, healer, and face morphologist. This book belongs in every home, school, and doctor's office."

ELIZABETH ANN MANHART BARRETT, PH.D., R.N., FAAN

"Reading this was like being back in Dr. Epstein's living room, studying with the master. Lamonica's unique brilliance lies in her ability to make face reading easy to understand, as she shares this ancient system with warmth and clarity. This book is a must-have addition to the bookshelf for anyone seeking to better understand themselves and others."

RANDY ELLEN KASPER, PH.D., LCSW,
AMERICAN INSTITUTE FOR MENTAL IMAGERY

"If you want to learn from the unbroken, unadulterated transmission of the millennia-old Western tradition of face reading, this is your book. Lamonica delivered a superbly crafted and illustrated manual that is well organized and easy to follow."

PETER S. REZNIK, PH.D., AUTHOR OF
FACE READING SECRETS FOR SUCCESSFUL RELATIONSHIPS

"This comprehensive and illustrated guide to the ancient and sacred art of face reading is masterfully laid out in a way that is clear, understandable, and so useful! This book is a tour de force and a must-read!"

PATRICIA PITTA, PH.D., ABPP

The
Art & Science
of Face Reading

Face Morphology in the
Western Spiritual
Tradition

Jennifer Lamonica, D.C., L.Ac., DACBN

Inner Traditions
Rochester, Vermont

Inner Traditions
One Park Street
Rochester, Vermont 05767
www.InnerTraditions.com

Text stock is SFI certified

Note to the reader: *This book is intended as an informational guide. The approaches and techniques described herein are meant to supplement, and not to be a substitute for, professional psychological or medical diagnosis and treatment.*

Cataloging-in-Publication Data for this title is available from the Library of Congress

ISBN 978-1-62055-877-5 (print)
ISBN 978-1-62055-878-2 (ebook)

Printed and bound in the United States by Lake Book Manufacturing, Inc. The text stock is SFI certified. The Sustainable Forestry Initiative® program promotes sustainable forest management.

10 9 8 7 6 5 4 3 2 1

Text design and layout by Virginia Scott Bowman
This book was typeset in Garamond Premier Pro with Jensen used as the display typeface
Illustrations on pages 39–41, 58, 59, 86, 99, 107, 112, 123, and 134 by Lindy Cacioppo
Illustrations on pages 56, 64–67, 71–73, 75–82, 91, 105, 110, 114, 119, 120–22, 124, 133, 135, and 143 by Dr. Rebbie Straubing
Photographs on pages 150–53 by Daniel Lamonica, model and photographer

To send correspondence to the author of this book, mail a first-class letter to the author c/o Inner Traditions • Bear & Company, One Park Street, Rochester, VT 05767, and we will forward the communication, or contact the author directly at **www.drlamonica.com.**

This book is dedicated to
the continuation of the work.

✦ ✦ ✦

The depth of the moment is eternity.
MADAME COLETTE ABOULKER-MUSCAT

Contents

Foreword

The year was 1985. I sat somewhat nervously, notebook on lap, surrounded by a group of my friends and colleagues, all waiting for our minds to be blown and our lives to be changed. The book-lined study of Dr. Gerald (Jerry) Epstein's New York City apartment was our launching pad, and we were all about to buckle up for a wild ride of information that would change the way we saw ourselves and each other, and the way we would come to help our patients.

As our group of chiropractors met, week after week, we all took in the information in our own way, as will all of you sitting in the classroom of this book. Well, that's not unusual. But what was new to us, and is probably new to you too, is that we were realizing that the ways we were different in how we were comprehending our lessons had less to do with things like our note-taking ability or study habits, and more to do with the shape of our nose or the depth of our philtrum (the vertical groove between the nose and the upper lip). What strange land had we stumbled upon? It was the ancient, sacred art of face morphology, and once you make the leap into this perspective, there is no turning back. Once you take the informal oath to look compassionately at all faces with a commitment to honor the sacred and unique expression that each face is, the world suddenly becomes populated with billions of reflections of the Infinite, all revealing their deep and complex nature right there on their face.

Well, that seminar series eventually ended and off we all went to use this material in our chiropractic practices. And as could easily have been predicted, one of us took this material and started using it with a confidence and level of mastery that could only bear the name Jennifer Lamonica. Jennifer is a phlegmatic Lymphatic, a morphological type that is a highly organized repository of information. In fact, when it comes to information that can help her help her patients, I would dare say she is insatiable. Over the years I have watched her study just about every chiropractic technique that crosses her path, and if she can use something she learned in a weekend seminar to help even one of her patients, well, few things make her happier than greeting that patient on Monday with a new way to take their healing even further.

I've watched her pore over journal after journal, clipping and filing research articles, nutritional discoveries, physiological breakthroughs, anything that represents a puzzle piece in her ever-evolving understanding of the miracle of the human body. I've watched her gather degrees and certificates (acupuncture, nutrition, mental imagery, etc.), all with such a natural and authentic desire to help people that unless you know Jennifer it is hard to imagine.

The funny thing is that she is so intuitive, all her vast knowledge and education act like mere iron filings in the magnetic field of her deep innate wisdom as a healer.

And so, as a face morphologist, when Jennifer looks at a face she sees everything she has ever studied revealed in the contours of that face's geometry. Whether a glance at a face points her to ask her patient questions about blood chemistry, marital status, joint pain, emotional upset, chronic infection, or anything else, you can pretty much trust it will lead to revelations that heal in a profound way.

About thirty-four years have passed since that first seminar in Jerry's apartment. And here we are. Jennifer has been called to the task, at the request of Dr. Epstein, of funneling this forty-five-hundred-year-old oral tradition into this book. She has painstakingly culled this material from thirty years of notes (many of which contain Zen koan–like statements that defy logical explanation). And so the book in your hands is a multilayered compendium. It has numerous invisible layers at its base, composed of millennia of esoteric oral tradition. It begins to come into focus with Madame Colette Aboulker-Muscat, taught by her father (and to my understanding this was unusual since she was a girl). Colette had extraordinary abilities that became evident at a young age. Another layer forms as Jerry leaves his conventional practice as a psychiatrist to follow Colette's teachings and to devote his professional life to helping his patients with this method. Which brings us to Jennifer's contribution: from my perspective, what Jennifer brings to this ancient river of teachings is heart, devotion, humility, and an uncanny talent as a healer.

REBBIE STRAUBING, D.C.

REBBIE STRAUBING is a chiropractor, the founder of the Yoga of Alignment (YOFA), author of *Rooted in the Infinite: The Yoga of Alignment,* and creator of two forms of remote energy work for people and animals: the YOFA *jhe* Sessions and YOFA Energy Sessions. A singer-songwriter who has created a body of spiritual chants for meditation and healing, she is also an animal communicator and practitioner of Ho'oponopono.

Preface

This book presents the details of an ancient system known as "face morphology," which reveals the secrets of the soul that are held within the structure of the face. My intention in compiling and sharing my understanding of this information is to enable you to have an objective awareness of your own personality, inclinations, and tendencies, both biological and psychological, and to provide practitioners with the means to help others gain a similar self-awareness.

I first learned about face morphology in 1985 from a chiropractic colleague of mine who had been having marital difficulties and had gone to Dr. Gerald Epstein, an accomplished proponent of both mental imagery and face morphology. Dr. Epstein read the faces of the couple and gave each of them new information about the other in a most compassionate and educative way. By coming to understand their facial structures, and what they represented, the couple was able to move past the judgments that each had held toward the other regarding specific behaviors. No other therapist had ever given them that type of aid, and my colleague was blown away. He and his wife stayed married, and he resolved to learn how to read faces to help his patients.

Dr. Epstein graciously invited him to organize a seminar for chiropractors at which he, Dr. Epstein, would teach the use of face morphology in the initial evaluation of a patient. I was invited to be a member of that first seminar series, and at the end of it, Dr. Epstein told us to go out and use what we had learned for seven years. And that is exactly what I did.

After seven years of practice, I contacted him and told him that I had been using the technique as instructed and asked, "Where do I go from here?" He invited me back to take classes at the institute that he had established—the American Institute of Mental Imagery, or AIMI. I studied with Dr. Epstein from 1992 to 2015, and he eventually granted me the distinction of Face Morphologist. My certification is through AIMI.

Dr. Gerald Epstein, of blessed memory, passed away in February 2019 before the publication of this book.

Over the years, I came to understand that face morphology was part of a tapestry of Western spiritual teachings that also included mental imagery and dreams. This information has been passed along from teacher to student and dates back forty-five hundred years, so it may be presumptuous to believe that any one individual can present the total content and intention of this God-given work. The energy of face morphology has been traveling through time like a sacred river; it has its own direction and will be received by those who are open to it. It is my humble honor to present my interpretation of what this river has given me, and I invite you to surf along yourself.

Acknowledgments

I would like to acknowledge the many players involved in the production of this work. First and foremost, Dr. Gerald Epstein, who introduced me to this sacred art and science via his dedication to teaching students this spiritual way of learning. He has influenced my life in so many ways and for this I am deeply grateful. He offered me a safe journey, on a path of light, to truth and self-awareness. This book represents the accumulation of information received at the foot of this master spanning more than three decades. I must also acknowledge, of course, his teacher Madame Colette Aboulker-Muscat for introducing him to this sacred system.

I would like to acknowledge my mother, Rose, and my father, Anthony, for giving me the opportunity to be here in this wonderful life. I want to also thank them for the wisdom and knowing that was passed along to me, not only genetically, but also in their honoring of God in a way that feels so right for me and so easy for me to feel and practice in my life.

I would like to acknowledge Dr. Rebbie Straubing for her marvelous contributions to this book. First, by saying, "Just write. You can worry about editing later. Just get it on the paper." I would also like to acknowledge her for her most wonderful illustrations and her tremendous contribution to editing. I thank her for always having my back and for her unswerving support and confidence in me in all the endeavors I have undertaken during our precious thirty-eight-year-long friendship.

A very special thank you goes to Lindy Cacioppo for her tireless hours of transcription and documentation and for being a trustworthy receptacle for all the components of this book as I gathered notes, thoughts, and insights that spanned decades. Her excellent technological savvy along with her contribution to editing were instrumental in bringing this book into tangible form.

I would also like to acknowledge my son, Daniel, for his excellent muscle control that enabled him to demonstrate the muscles of the mouth, and for simply giving me the opportunity to be the mother of such a wonderful son—and how great is that? I would like to acknowledge Rachel Epstein for all her encouragement and help. And a warm thank you to all my patients.

Most of all I would like to acknowledge God for allowing this sacred art and science to be revealed to us.

◆ ◆ ◆

The true being
Is there
Among us;
Divided into creatures
In every other face
I recognize Him,
And I see me!

COLETTE ABOULKER-MUSCAT,
A POEM SHE GAVE TO
DR. GERALD EPSTEIN

◆ ◆ ◆

Foundation in the Basics

The practice of face morphology has changed my life. For more than three decades, I have had the distinct privilege of evaluating patients using the ancient, sacred art of face morphology, or *face reading,* as it is often called. Finding meaning hidden in the body is not new to us. In the 1960s, books on "body language" were all the rage, but as I came to see, body language is an observation of morphology. And as far as I am concerned, morphology falls under the category of sacred geometry, which has very personal meaning to me.

As a child, access to mathematical understanding was always there for me in the form of geometric shapes—and still is today. For example, when I meditate and I see out of my third eye, what I see is a series of triangles, perhaps a portal into different dimensions. A system of triangles was also revealed to me when I studied the body in chiropractic school. The revelation that the pelvis and the sacrum form the base of a triangle that has its apex at the twelfth thoracic vertebra, and that the shoulders contribute a similar downward pointing triangle, has translated into many back pains alleviated.

When I was a student, I simply accepted these images as something that fit my way of thinking. Then one day we were in a class called Logan Basic, and I realized that the triangles I was seeing in my inner eye were also *diagrammed in the textbook.* What I saw in my mind was there on the page! That is when I understood that what I saw with the inner eye was a known principle of the sacred geometry of the body.

And the geometry of the face takes this one step further. When decoded, it tells us how we interface with the world. You could say that the face is made of geometry, and so morphology is a form of geometry—a tangible sacred geometry. We have a variety of forms of access to divine truths through different portals. Sacred geometry is one of them. It is an Egyptian donation to our culture, and I believe morphology comes to us through a similar portal.

The understanding of faces is ancient. Face morphology derives from the Western spiritual tradition of both the inner image of mental imagery and the outer image of the face. It is passed along in the lineage of Madame Colette Aboulker-Muscat to Dr. Gerald Epstein and on to me and his other students.

Most relevant to us in its written record is the section on face reading in the Kabbalah, the chief text of Jewish mysticism, written by Rabbi Akiva, and the Zohar, which was written by his student, Rabbi Shimon Bar-Yochai.

The Kabbalah is presented as an allegorical interpretation of the Pentateuch, which composes the first five books of Moses within the written Hebrew Scriptures (which are also known as the Bible). There are two forms of the Bible. One is the written Bible, also known as the Old and New Testaments, and the other is the mystical aspect of the Bible that was only taught in an oral tradition. Dr. Epstein taught that there are more than four hundred references to the face in the Bible.

In the Zohar, it is written that the rabbis looked at the vein patterns on the face and saw letters in Hebrew. From this they understood how the face had an effect on the world and how the world had an effect upon the face. This view of faces, passed from teacher to student since the time of the prophets, is the foundation of the material that follows in this book.

This system of face reading, which is mostly taught in Europe, especially in France, is a Western spiritual tradition, and was passed from teacher to student as the major diagnostic system until the middle of the fifteenth century. *Complexio,* a medical practice that included face morphology as the diagnostic component and mental imagery as the treatment, was practiced during the late Middle Ages up through the mid-Renaissance. While complexio was disbanded and the modern practice of medicine changed, French medical schools still have morphological classes in their anatomy and surgical curricula to determine the appropriateness of plastic surgery in each individual case. Even in the French business world, there is an understanding of face morphology.

Other cultures have their own approaches. The Chinese look at the patient's face to understand the physiology within. The Ayurvedic and Russian systems often look at body types. The Italians understand diagnosing through the face and represent archetypes in their art. As Dr. Epstein taught, the Hermetic and Greek traditions are rooted in the belief that "your fulfillment lies in living out what your face shows. Hence, the Greek's use of exquisite sculptures of the gods and goddesses (imitated in the Roman pantheon) to remind the populace of their likenesses to those prototypical beings, each of whom bore essential characteristics to be lived out by human beings bearing the similar-looking face."

While each culture tends to have a primary morphological type, in today's homogenized world, it no longer always fits. As we can see in the United States and elsewhere, many morphological types have mated to create mixtures that are not as easily recognized. We must adapt our morphological reading now to compensate for this evolution.

The system of face morphology I use in this book is based on the Caucasian race. I was taught that this system is specific to Caucasian features and that we are unable to use it to read the features of other races. However, there are so many other morphological traits, other than the specific features, that can be read considering the profile and the front-face, that I believe that much of this Caucasian system can be used in all races. I also believe that ethnic differences, which ultimately arise because of different climate-influenced survival adaptations, can be interpreted. For many years, I have been reading the faces of people who come from other cultures, and it has proven effective. For this reason, it is my strong opinion that we can identify inherited feature attributes within race adaptations.

For example, in Caucasian faces, eyes indicate many things based on attributes such as size, color, shape, slant, and positioning. These variations clearly speak to variations in temperament, personality, and health. This might bring one to think that, for example, almond-shaped Asian eyes would have the same interpretation as almond-shaped Caucasian eyes, but this is not so. There are, however, many other features of the Asian face that can be interpreted and fit into the Caucasian system. I believe that with practice, we can interpret the slight variations within other races and read the face as accurately as we can with Caucasians.

The Art of Face Morphology

You may be wondering at this point how face morphology can be used to help us in our everyday lives. My mentor, Dr. Gerald Epstein, provides an answer: "Morphology is the key that allows you entry into a whole world of informational knowledge about yourself and others." When you enter this morphological perspective, you can discover a whole host of useful understandings, including your natural characteristics; your optimal career; the kind of partner that is most compatible with your type; the diet, exercise, vitamins, and minerals that are best for you; and where you would be most comfortable living. You can even gain insight into the best ways to raise your child based on your child's morphology. In addition, you will become aware of the best ways to prevent illness and maintain health for yourself based on your own morphology.

When exploring what is normal and natural for you, it is important to note that in face morphology there are no categories aimed at pigeonholing you or designating you as *abnormal* or suffering from pathology.

Face morphology doesn't classify or compare you to a supposed norm; it is purely descriptive and has no preferences, judgments, or prejudices. You simply are what your face reveals.

Even though we are all made in the image and likeness of our Source, we recognize our differences. Removing all value judgments and knowing that no one can really be *better* than another, we can only be different by our faces. This was a great revelation to me, when Dr. Epstein pointed out that "We are not different from each other in kind, as the authoritarian institutions would have us believe, making some people automatically *better* than others *beneath* them. Rather we are different simply by what our faces show. We are different from each other in degree at the least, and just plain different by face alone."

Dr. Epstein continually reiterated that there was no comparison of one individual to another. This is a compassionate, descriptive science and art with no biases built into it. The next level of that is that since there are no standards or ideals, the burden of guilt feelings and anxiety is lifted, giving the person an immediate sense of relief and freedom.

Given these benefits, it is easy to see the great impact face morphology can have on self-healing. In addition, for a healing practitioner with training in face morphology, by accurately interpreting what is shown on a patient's face, he or she can better understand what might be causing a particular ailment or issue and then help to alleviate it. As Dr. Epstein put it: "With [face morphology] we get to the heart of the matter clinically in short order. We don't waste time. Instead, we give the sufferer what his or her face shows us is needed. Beneficial shifts begin taking place immediately."

What's in a Face?

I have come to accept the belief that the soul is eternal, and it is each soul's choice to incarnate. In so doing, the soul chooses its parents to get the best blueprint of the face. The belief that the soul is eternal also entails the understanding that by choosing the faces of the parents, one chooses one's own path, inclinations, tendencies, and personality. The face is the representation of the DNA sequencing of each human being. While each face is unique, it contains a collection of inherited ancestral tendencies, and it is through these tendencies, passed along from antiquity, that men and women live their days here on Earth. In every moment we have the opportunity to have earthly experiences that either enrich or deny our familial predispositions.

It is stated in Deuteronomy that the errors of the ancestors are carried to the fourth generation and that a blessing can reverse those errors by moral action. So we can literally bless ourselves and our ancestors and progeny by correcting familial errors, inclinations, and tendencies through our actions in life.

For example, let us say that a child has an ancestral tendency toward theft but is educated morally and learns that it is incorrect to steal. Every time the impulse is thwarted, there is a blessing. Through this understanding we can begin to find the hidden blessings in even our greatest challenges. God put within us a plan to enlighten our being and enrich our soul while making a journey through this college called Earth.

In the ancient sacred art of face morphology, we understand that there is the law of reciprocity. This law states that the face, as expressed on the outside, literally reflects what is happening on the inside, and that what is happening on the inside also reflects what is on the face. For instance, when viewing the face of someone who is bitter, you will observe a frown. And conversely, if someone holds their face in a frown, it will create an inner state of bitterness. Similarly, a happy person will exhibit a mild smile even when the face is relaxed, and by lifting the edges of the mouth into a smile with the fingers, a depressed person can cultivate an inner state of happiness.

These observations are not limited to mood and emotions. For example, if a person is missing the lateral third of the eyebrow, it means that the person has a thyroid condition. (I will explain the three parts of the eyebrow in a later section.) And conversely, by removing the lateral third of the eyebrow, a person will disturb their otherwise normal thyroid functions.

What these examples show us is of great significance in the practical application of face morphology. They highlight the fact that just as a person's external behavior interfaces with the world, so does the face. As the person reacts to the world, the front-face changes; as the front-face changes, the internal physiology reacts.

Infants, who have not yet been exposed to the world, have a fresh opportunity to have all of their experiences, social interactions, climate effects, and moral suggestions impregnated onto their front-face. There is a deep lesson here for parents. According to Dr. Epstein, infants, at the time of birth, have 95 percent of their qualities in place. We can see during their lifetime that their face reveals an unfolding of all their traits and their morphological inclinations—in other words, their fixed traits emerge.* For example, if a Lymphatic child is sprayed with cold water from a hose or lawn sprinkler on a hot summer day, she will most likely giggle with delight and record that as a fun and happy experience. The same aged Nervous child might run away crying and record that as a trauma. These experiences will influence the face in completely different ways according to the underlying temperament that has been set in place from birth. Unfortunately, parents often try to raise their children from a general psychological point of view without regard for the specifics of each child's type.

The fact is, there has never before been, nor will there ever be, another face like yours. Your face is unique and incomparable. It reflects your direction in life and points to your individual way of fulfillment. Dr. Epstein also pointed out that the Talmud, two thousand years ago, expressed that there are as many paths as there are faces. Every face is

---

*Until bony ossification is complete, at about twenty-five years old, the profile changes. But after that it is a fixity and the temperament stays the same until a fleshy overgrowth typically obscures the bony mandible, which usually happens after age sixty-five.

unique and each person's path is unique. There are no standards and ideals that are the basis for any individual face. That is why face reading is such a compassionate act. It brings an understanding of all the qualities with which one is born, and it removes all the guilt feelings regarding the presumed impact of social, logical, and psychological standards and ideals. What is more, each morphological type has its own proclivity toward eating, mating, and health, and each type is honored for its unique qualities.

Face morphology also assists us in making unbiased and useful observations of the changes in loved ones, family members, and friends. Many of us come to such learning intuitively. We do it all the time whenever we gaze into the eyes of another. For instance, when a parent looks into the eyes of his or her own newborn baby, there is an instant yoking, perhaps even a soul bonding. When infants look into the eyes of their parents, again there is an instantaneous yoking. When we encounter someone ominous, the opposite occurs just as naturally. One can actually feel a sense of repulsion or distaste when gazing at a face that feels threatening.

As the Bible states, we have been made in the likeness and image of our Creator. We look to the Creator as a parent, and our Creator has given us human counterparts that are also made in God's likeness and image. Therefore, we yoke ourselves to our human counterparts as an indirect pathway to the Divine. In daily life, we act instinctively in response to how we perceive the faces we encounter. In fact, this innate facial recognition is mapped in the brain by neuroscientists.

The Practice of Face Morphology

Because this practice is a sacred art, care must be given when *reading* an individual. It is important to get the permission of the individual before reading and reporting what you see in his or her morphology. During the course of my practice I've received permission from the majority of my patients to read their faces, usually as part of my initial examination.

Here is a surprising example from the very early days in my face morphology career.

A Surprising Revelation

One day a new patient walked into my office. I greeted her and brought her in for an examination. I asked her for permission to read her face, since it would help me to understand her problem. I also explained to her a little bit about face morphology. She heartily gave me permission to read her face, which most patients do, since everyone is interested in learning about themselves. Within a few minutes this is what came blurting out of my mouth: "Who did you murder?" I had taken a leap in trusting what her face was telling me, but I did not expect the answer that she gave. She said, "My husband." And of course, as I could see that she was in my office and not in prison, the judge had obviously deemed it to be self-defense.

From that point forward, I began to see the rich efficacy of face reading. I've experienced countless other revelations with patients over the years that have allowed me to help them deepen their understanding of themselves.

Here is an example of my reading of a woman from another culture.

Persian Royalty

I had a patient who I knew right away had to be Persian, even though her family is from another area. She is also married to someone from a different country. But when I looked at her and asked her if she was Persian, she said, "Yes." I went a step further and asked, "Are you Persian royalty?" and she said, "Yes." It was in the morphology of her nose and actually in her feet. Her second toe was elongated, which is a morphological characteristic of Persian royalty and is also pharaonic (pertaining to a pharaoh).

In moments like these, I feel so honored to be able to converse with people and deepen my understanding as well as their self-awareness. I think it changes the nature of the visit. When patients feel acknowledged, they can feel the freedom to reveal themselves. Face morphology helps us know ourselves on a deeper level, which opens us to a direct relationship with God and the beautiful exchange that goes with that. To paraphrase several traditions, one might say, "To know God is to know thyself, and to know thyself is to know God."

What a wonderful opportunity we have to know ourselves through the ancient, sacred art of face morphology. And since repetition has proven to be the best way to learn, the art, science, and philosophy of face morphology will be presented in different contexts throughout this book.

About This Book

In this book, I often refer to the faces of famous people as examples. Since they have put themselves in the public eye, they have in effect given us permission to look at them, and by doing so, we can see and learn from faces that are common in our experience. Please note that we are in no way diagnosing or attributing any emotional or personality characteristics to these people; we are only looking at them for examples of geometric shapes and pointing out features for ease of recognition.

It is also important to note that some of the statements in this book may seem bold or strong by assigning a certain (sometimes challenging) characteristic to a certain face or feature. I want to take a moment to address this as an umbrella statement to cover this issue across the board, in this whole book. It is my aim to present this material in a manner that is true to the way it was taught to me, and so I pass along to you the clarity and definitiveness of this system. As you read this, please be aware that while a certain aspect of the face might indicate brutality, or some other extremely unwanted characteristic of the personality, these aspects are often tempered by other compensating morphological characteristics in the same face. Also, intelligence shows up in many different ways on the face, so please be aware that if I describe a certain aspect of a feature as a sign of more or less intelligence, there may be other aspects of that same face that counterbalance or enhance that aspect.

Part of the art of being a true morphologist is in compassionately reading all the relationships, interactions, and levels of meaning in the face—what you might even think of as the chemistry of the face. Each face presents a complex set of checks and balances that, interestingly enough, we aim to read quickly and intuitively—a paradox perhaps, but this is where the mastery comes in. So please understand as you read this book that each seemingly bold statement you may encounter here is one piece of the puzzle and must be considered within the context of the whole for the benefit and self-revelation of the person whose soul chose that face for this lifetime.

Also be aware that any of the gender-specific gestures that are noted in this book can be applicable to all genders. The language and examples presented were taught to me from a time when gender stereotypes were more prevalent.

This book is organized in a way that moves from general to specific. We begin with an introduction to the four temperaments: Bilious, Nervous, Sanguine, and Lymphatic. The view that there are four temperaments comes from the Old Testament. Ezekiel was a prophet who was shown a vision of a chariot. The chariot had four posts, and each post had the faces of four creatures—a lion, an eagle, an ox, and an angel. Each creature represents a temperament: the angel (also known as angel/man) represents the Bilious, the eagle represents the Nervous, the lion represents the Sanguine, and the ox represents the Lymphatic. These terms may sound odd to you, but they soon will become familiar.

I believe it is also worth noting that in the Western spiritual life, *four* has the meaning of construction, that is, of coming into being. In Hebrew, four letters (one is repeated)—*yod, hay, vav,* and *hay*—form the tetragrammaton, which represents the creation of man. Then there are the four flows of rivers—the Gihon, Euphrates, Tigris, and Pishon—which in Israel represent the movement of human life from its source.

We also see the number four in the apostles—the French call them archangels—of the New Testament: Matthew is the man or angel in human form and is Bilious, John is the eagle and Nervous, Mark is the lion and Sanguine, and Luke is the ox and Lymphatic.

All these sets of fours are in a sense the same fours. We shall continue to see them as we advance in our journey into face morphology. As our study progresses, the four temperaments will be visited again and again as we include more details about each one.

1

Reading the Profile

The study of face morphology largely refers to the bony structure of the face, which is inherited. When discussing face morphology, which is read in layers, we begin with the profile to determine what we refer to as the "temperament." There are four temperaments defined in face morphology: Bilious, Nervous, Sanguine, and Lymphatic. The Bilious and the Sanguine are considered active, and the Nervous and the Lymphatic are considered passive. In figure 1.1 on the following page, you can see that the temperaments on the left side are active, and those on the right side are passive.

In this chapter, we examine the four temperaments, each of which is analogous to one of the faces of the four creatures on each of the four posts in Ezekiel's vision, which was mentioned in the introduction. It bears repeating that the Bilious temperament represents the angel/man, the Nervous the eagle, the Sanguine the lion, and the Lymphatic the ox. In the pages ahead, short lists introduce each of the four temperaments. In these lists I highlight some of the foremost features of people with that particular temperament. In my discussion, I also describe some of the common health problems of each temperament and how the problems are most effectively treated. It is important to note that although the nutritional recommendations for morphological types are accurate for the type, every person is an individual and must consult their nutritionist or other health-care practitioner for appropriate dosing and possible contraindications.

I hasten to add, however, that we each have *all* four temperaments,

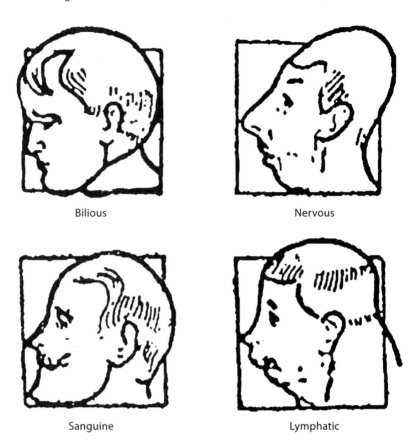

Bilious

Nervous

Sanguine

Lymphatic

Fig. 1.1. The four temperaments

even though the primary one represents our predominant characteristics (along with our strengths and/or weaknesses) and the others our secondary, tertiary, and quaternary qualities. Further, we all live by a twenty-four-hour clock, and there are particular times in the day, defined as quaternary, whereby a person can have the most benefit from his or her own temperament.

I would also add here that although this is not a book on embryology, certain terms will be used that may not be familiar to you. So as a quick reference: after a sperm meets an egg, that fertilized egg, or zygote, continues to divide and develops into an embryo in layers. We recognize these layers as the endoderm, the mesoderm, and the ectoderm, which is divided into two layers—anterior and posterior.

This has been known since ancient times. As described by Hippocrates in somewhat more formal language, during development, each of the four temperaments has the predominance of one layer of the human embryo over the other. Each temperament, according to Hippocrates, is represented by an anterior ectodermal layer, a posterior ectodermal layer, a mesodermal layer, and an endodermal layer. In fact, each of us has all four embryological layers; however, again, one is primary while the others take secondary, tertiary, and quaternary positions. These terms will become clearer in our profiles of the four temperaments.

The Bilious Profile

We begin with the Bilious temperament, which is the only temperament that shares two layers of the four dermal derivations. The Bilious type derives from the chordoblast (a combination of mesodermal and ectodermal layers) and the ectoblast (ectodermal layer). As with all the temperaments, I open with brief notes on major characteristics of the Bilious type to familiarize you with the particular quarter of the day, the season, and the disposition that are most relevant to the personality and activity of this type.

When reading the Bilious profile from the left side, as is the convention, notice that the forehead can be pouched forward like the shape of a reverse question mark. The range from an extreme pouch to a lesser pouch and all the way to a straight line from the nasal bridge to the hairline is included in the Bilious profile. The jawline (the outline of the mandible from the ear to the chin) comes down about two-thirds of the way to the chin, and the back of the head is like a bowling ball.

Characteristics of the Bilious Temperament

- **Prime embryological layers:** Chordoblast and ectoblast
- **Season:** Summer
- **Disposition:** The Bilious has harmony with other people.
- **Daily quaternary:** 6:00 p.m.–12:00 a.m. is when the tissue associated with the Bilious temperament is nourished and strong.
- **Sleep:** The amount of activity does not affect sleep. The Bilious does not need much sleep and can sleep under any conditions.
- **Skin tone:** Brown

Bilious types have an active, intellectual, objective outlook. They seek the actual and the concrete and are effective gatherers of knowledge. They are constructors, and they make things happen. They also may be willing to stretch the truth to serve their plan.

The Bilious are a chordoblastic, medium-built people. They frequently have black hair on their head, which tends to look like a bowling ball from the back, and the palms of their hands are often darkly complected. They have short, compact muscles and need to be physical. Those with a Bilious temperament are considered to be beautiful swarthy people, befitting the expression "tall, dark, and handsome," and may have a Casanova look (see figure 1.2). Many Italians are of the Bilious type.

One should not try to antagonize the Bilious as they may hold a grudge. Taken to their extreme, they wish to conquer the world or become dictators. Hitler, Mussolini, and Genghis Khan were all Bilious types, as were Napoleon and Casanova.

Fig. 1.2. Giacomo Girolamo Casanova

The Bilious types prefer cold, wet environments. They need chlorophyll for oxygenation, and they need ozone. They have a great ability to utilize oxygen and burn it, which makes them excellent marathon runners. They also have plenty of stamina to keep them going, and they do not like to rest. Bilious types are very impatient with pain, and they tend to have more bone problems than do the other three temperaments.

The Bilious temperament likes a challenge and enjoys being victorious. Due to their strong will, they can sometimes exact claims and power over other people, which can be difficult in relationships with people of a more passive type. When the will of the Bilious is not met, they can experience depression.

Bilious thinking is not abstract; it is concrete, constructive, coordinated, controlled, and organized, and the Bilious like things to be done to their exact wishes. They cast a very calm demeanor, while their wheels are turning inside, calculating and planning but not revealing their intellective power. Due to the critical thinking and strong mental capabilities of the Bilious type, obstacles are fun for them to overcome. The Bilious approach challenges as mental puzzles to solve. Their mental and physical prowess also allows them to be successful in most of their endeavors, but it can tend to make them difficult bosses, expecting others to have the same abilities.

Because of their critical nature, it can be difficult for Bilious people to have relationships with one another, and jealousy is often associated with this type. If you try to thwart the Bilious, there will be problems in the relationship. They will become morose and brooding and can seek vengeance. Bilious types get along well with Lymphatics, as the Lymphatic type is more tolerant. On the other hand, the Bilious are not a good match for Nervous types because they are not forthcoming with the admiration and adoration that Nervous types need.

Bilious types can be interested in the past and can tend to hoard money, and professionally many choose to be psychotherapists of all types.

Anatomically, Bilious people tend to have a medium-length digestive tract, and therefore, abusive diets can lead to weakness in the alimentary canal. While they are omnivores, they would do well to protect themselves by reducing their input of red meat, poultry, lamb, and root vegetables. The Mediterranean diet, with fish, grains, leafy green vegetables, and a moderate amount of protein, is good for this type, especially since they need a lot of ozone, and these foods are rich in oxygen.

As noted at the outset in the list of Bilious characteristics, the key embryological layers are the chordoblast and ectoblast. The chordoblast is a combination of mesodermal and ectodermal layers that gives rise to eyes, ears, bones, the epithelium of the lungs, and organs of the body, including the gallbladder and liver. The part of the Bilious temperament that is ectoblast gives rise to the lens of the eye, the ears, tooth enamel, salivary glands, adrenal glands, bones, and ligaments. So when we speak about Bilious types and the weaknesses they might have, we have to look to these particular systems.

The Bilious generally have to be careful about bone and ligament troubles. They tend toward osteopenia, which is a decrease in bone density, and osteoporosis, which is a more advanced state that occurs with aging where the bones actually start to develop holes. When evaluating these people, also look at the joints. Sacroiliac ligaments can become weakened, especially if the person engages in long-distance running, which is common for the type.

The Bilious temperament is associated with the flow of bile; therefore, gallstones may be a difficulty. Since Bilious types tend toward liver problems, care should be given with regard to fat soluble vitamins (A, D, E, K), so beta carotene, being water soluble, is better for them than vitamin A. Similarly, should a Bilious develop diabetes, one would look to the glycogen storage function of the liver.

Overall Bilious types tend to be healthy, but when they go for general lab tests, it is important for them to include tests such as SGOT (serum glutamic oxaloacetic acid transaminase) also known as AST (aspartate aminotransferase), SGPT (serum glutamic pyruvate transaminase) also known as ALT (alanine aminotransferase), GGTP (gamma-glutamyl transpeptidase), and indirect bilirubin, as these will reveal liver problems if they are elevated.

When looking at the complete blood count of a Bilious, we generally notice that the proportion of lymphocytes to segmented cells (known as polymorphonuclear white cells) is more even than in the other types. When the Bilious are under stress, their overall white blood cell count can become low.

Bilious, you may recall, is associated with the angel/man in Ezekiel's chariot. The Bilious are indefatigable, they can acquire huge amounts of information, and they need little sleep.

Woman with Reconstructive Surgery

I couldn't read the morphology of one of my female patients. It was very strange to me. She presented with symptoms that did not make sense based on my reading of her profile. When I questioned her, she explained that she had had reconstructive surgery on her skull because she had been in a severe accident. Now as a result, she did not have normal cranial sutures. The bones were flapped over each other, and the scalp and hair grew sparsely over the scars. On one side of her head she was Bilious, and on the other side she was not. It was a very strange thing. I told her I was having difficulty reading her profile, and she said, "Oh, let me show you my good one." She turned to the other side, and when I saw that profile, I realized the extent of the movement and reconstruction the bones of her face and skull had undergone. Because the bony structure had been changed, the morphology of her "good side" had also been changed, and the complications that arose from this accident had an effect on her symptomatology.

The Nervous Profile

When reading the Nervous profile, notice that the forehead slopes back and the chin slopes back making a sideways *V*. The line from the ear to the chin is straight, and the back of the head is bullet-shaped. A profile cast as an arrowhead is a vivid example of a Nervous profile. Note that the profile diagrams are drawn as exaggerations to make this point. When viewing the profile, the line of energy flow is toward the top back of the head.

Characteristics of the Nervous Temperament

- **Prime embryological layer:** Ectoderm
- **Season:** Autumn
- **Disposition:** The Nervous has determination.
- **Daily quaternary:** 12:00 p.m.–6:00 p.m. is when the tissue

associated with the Nervous temperament is nourished and strong.

- **Sleep:** The Nervous can sleep during the day and may be prone to insomnia at night.
- **Skin tone:** Yellow

The temperament of the Nervous type is passive, abstract, intellectual, and subjective, almost entirely the opposite of the Bilious. The Nervous temperament is associated with electricity. Nervous types have the shortest digestive tract of all four temperaments and are the true vegetarians. They do not do well when they eat meat, as a longer digestive tract is necessary to digest the heavier protein. They do better eating six to eight small meals per day, rather than a few big meals.

Emotionally, the personality of the Nervous needs many of what we call the *A's:* adoration, adulation, admiration, attention, applause, acclaim, acceptance, and acknowledgment. The three most commonly used descriptors are adoration, adulation, and admiration. Perhaps this is why most show business performers are the Nervous type. This leads them to seek the spotlight.

Nervous types can easily get depressed when not admired. In relationships, if they do not receive these *A's,* they are likely to leave. They thrive on stimulation from the outside world. Their life is motivated by what others think of them and how others respond to them. You must give to them before they can give to you.

More broadly, those with the Nervous temperament may have trouble coping with life due to the fact that everything seems like a burden to them. When they grow older, the importance they place on what others think about them can become extremely troubling.

Professionally, Nervous types have a very strong ability to assess the moment-to-moment changes of the stock market. Because of the quick movement of their minds, they are able to grasp the moment, and they like to play with high-risk investments. They tend to exaggerate, and they like to tell long, involved stories that embellish the facts they perceive. They also tend to be hyperreactive, often misunderstood as being hyperemotional.

Due to their expressive nature and the ectomorphic thinness of their body, Nervous types are often misperceived as deeply feeling. But as compared to the other passive type, the endomorphic Lymphatic type that has the ability to store feelings and feel deeply, we see that the Nervous type is more expressive than deeply feeling. This distinction is characteristic of the Nervous, and as a practitioner, you can help them by giving them mental exercises to develop patience. They learn this by adopting a practice of waiting before they discharge their emotions.

The Nervous are abstract thinkers and are bored easily. They often have great ideas, but, being a passive type, they do not have the physical energy to carry them out. They have only short bursts of energy. This is the reason they need a partner with the energy to execute their ideas. Nervous types always seek out new sense impressions. As a practitioner, you must avoid shocking them and try to bring them gently to your discoveries.

Given their short bursts of energy, good activities for the Nervous type are tap dancing, gymnastics, fencing, and ice-skating. Nervous types do not do well with heavy aerobic exercise, because as they breathe heavily they will expel too much carbon dioxide, which is the gas that they need most. If they expel too much carbon dioxide too quickly they may faint.

Nervous types often have a strong projecting nose on profile. They need that nose as an anchor, and they use it to pierce the world. It is also needed to compensate for their lack of a chin. The profile of the Nervous type has a chin that projects backward. If the nose is shortened or if the bump between the cartilage and bony structure in the middle of the nose is removed, their hyperreactivity to external stimuli may also be removed. The Nervous type can suffer by becoming too passive and depressed.

Nervous individuals frequently want to have rhinoplasty. If you are in a position to council these people, consider making them aware that a flatter nose can prohibit them from successfully engaging with or *piercing* the world. This information might encourage them to leave their nose as is. Nervous types who have already undergone such an alteration may notice personality changes such as depression and beyond. In France, plastic surgeons consult with face morphologists before plastic surgery to avoid such psychological difficulties. Changing the nose can also cause a loss of strength and sexuality.

If people with a Nervous temperament present to you that they have difficulty calming themselves, beneficial nutrients such as vitamin B_1 and magnesium can prove very helpful. The titration of these nutrients would start with 100 milligrams of B_1 and go up to 1,200 milligrams, as needed, in hundred-milligram increments. With magnesium, you could start at 500 milligrams and work your way up to 1,500 milligrams. In general, the primary Nervous type needs vitamins B_1 and B_2 and chelated magnesium.

A Mismatched Chin

I have a patient who is a very gentle Nervous, but his chin doesn't really recede. I said to him, "Your physical nature and the symptoms that you have correlate with the Nervous, but your profile doesn't really match it." He said, "I had a chin job." He had an implant that tempered the Nervous temperament. And since he had had the chin job, he had become more athletic, sports oriented, and a motorcycle rider as well.

The Nervous temperament can also be prone to hypochondriasis. Even so, they tend to live the longest of the four temperament types.

Embryologically, this type is associated with problems of the skin and the nervous system. These individuals can have skin lesions and rashes in their early years. Especially when an adult Nervous type develops neurological symptoms, take heed, because it is probably nervous system related. The Nervous type's strengths and weaknesses are primarily concerned with the peripheral and central nervous system. The organs that can be affected, derived from the ectoderm, include the brain, the spinal cord, the spinal nerves, the skin, the mouth cavity, teeth enamel, the salivary glands, the buccal lining, the nasal lining, part of the pharynx, part of the sinuses, the hypothalamus, the anal epithelium, the distal urethra, the adrenal medulla, the epidermis, hair, nails, sebaceous and sweat glands, the lens of the eye, the conjunctiva, the retina, and the internal and external ear.

The patient may present to the practitioner a symptom that only represents the most surface layers of a health issue. By understanding morphology we may be able to identify the underlying layers of dysfunction that have contributed to the manifestation of that symptom. Meanwhile, the body has been piling layer upon layer of adaptations that are covering the core issue.

As we understand that a Nervous type's weakness and strength is the nervous system, we want to turn our attention to nervous system conditions when this type presents with issues such as epilepsy or adrenal medulla insufficiency.

If a patient with the Nervous temperament comes in with a headache, we must suspect the brain, even though headaches may derive from vascular components or a plethora of other causes. Knowing that the person is of the Nervous temperament can clue us in to the fact that there may be nervous system involvement. Lab work is helpful in this situation. We must look at the levels of calcium, magnesium, and electrolytes in these cases. A delicately balanced environment is necessary for normal synaptic firing to occur in the brain.

If a Nervous type becomes depressed, as can frequently occur, we may have to look at neurotransmitter levels, especially serotonin. Of course, there are social factors that can contribute to depression that should be observed in all types; however, it appears to be commonplace that the Nervous type can have neurotransmitter strengths and weaknesses. With other types, we would look elsewhere.

The Sanguine Profile

When reading the Sanguine profile, notice that the forehead is sloped back, the jawline is at or near 90°, and the back of the head is like a spatula.

Characteristics of the Sanguine Temperament

- **Prime embryological layer:** Mesoderm
- **Season:** Spring
- **Disposition:** The Sanguine has energy.
- **Daily quaternary:** 6:00 a.m.–12:00 noon is when the tissue associated with the Sanguine temperament is nourished and strong.
- **Sleep:** The Sanguine may enjoy a nap after a large meal.
- **Skin tone:** Red

Sanguine types are active, corporeal, and highly subjective—that is, concerned with direct experience. They have strong jaws, like Dick Tracy and the American-type man often typified by Ronald Reagan and Paul Newman.

Sanguine types can be thought of as gladiators; they are very muscular—the most muscular of the four temperaments—and they love to exercise. They build muscle easily and therefore can excel at weight lifting. They also love high-impact aerobic exercise and are very good at hockey, rugby, wrestling, and indeed, any aggressive sport, including the martial arts. Due to their ability to thrust forward easily, they especially excel in football. Given their need for activity, Sanguine types should engage in at least one hour of exercise per day.

The Sanguine is task oriented. You might say that the United States is a Sanguine nation, as the Sanguine nature is to be strong and glorious and to work hard. However, it is not usually Sanguine style to keep working all day long. In fact, after a period of hard work they have to rest, like the lion that represents them in Ezekiel's vision. In general, Sanguine types need a good amount of sleep—eight to ten hours per day—and should have a nap during the day to recharge their batteries.

People with a Sanguine temperament tend to love beautiful material things and be most comfortable in a climate that is cold and dry, which is why they often need dehumidifiers. They are gregarious and tend to be optimistic, extroverted, and quite social. They like to connect with other people and enjoy having many in their group of friends and family, just as the lion has many in its pride. Also like the lion, the Sanguine tend to be territorial. John Wayne is a good example of this temperament.

Because they are easily distracted, Sanguine types have difficulty being punctual. While they intend to be in the moment, they often grow impatient because they do not have long attention spans. Most of them have difficulty sitting still (they need action) and can be viewed as being hyperactive or perhaps as having an attention deficit. In their need for movement and action, they don't stay with one task for a long while and therefore are labeled as having a short attention span. They are also known for their outbursts of temper. They are truly the physical motoric type. Even though they are always on the move, the Sanguine can be very analytical and enjoy being scientists.

People with the Sanguine temperament are also strong-headed. Willing and quick to remove physical obstacles, they do not stop to think their way around things. In fact, due to their daredevil nature and their impetuousness, their activity can lead to overly aggressive behavior.

Sanguine types have the second longest digestive tract and do very well on three square meals a day, without snacking between meals. While they can use moderate amounts of liquid and small amounts of vegetables and fruits, they must eat meat, which provides the large amounts of protein and full complement of the amino acids necessary for muscle building. If they try vegetarianism, they may become weak, tired, irritable, and experience loss of muscle. Sanguines who do attempt vegetarianism often admit that they miss eating meat.

The Sanguine temperament is associated with blood and the color red. Sanguines need blood, which is usually derived from red meat, and they often have a ruddy facial complexion and reddish palms. It is significant that blood is both their strength and their weakness. If a Sanguine has a disorder, it is likely to be an imbalance of the blood or a severe infection in the blood, vascular system, and/or possibly the heart.

Sanguine types rarely get depressed. Instead, their problems tend to be muscular and circulatory in nature. They are off their game when their muscles are not working, but when their muscles are healthy and strong, so are their hearts. However, if Sanguines are out of balance, their hearts can be affected.

Because the Sanguine types enjoy a lot of exercise, they can accumulate lactic acid after their physical motoric activities. Under certain conditions this can lead to trigger points—neuromuscular accumulations of lactic acid and inflammatory proteins that create muscular pain. Being the muscular motoric type, Sanguines enjoy massage. Pressing into these trigger points brings them great relief.

If Sanguine types do not receive enough fluid—about a quart a day per fifty pounds of body weight—the lactic acid concentration accumulates, trigger points increase, and there is a proclivity toward muscular dysfunction. Since Sanguine strength and weakness depend on blood and muscle, an important lab test to examine is the enzyme CPK (creatine phosphokinase), which can increase with high muscle activity.

Sanguine activity can bring other physical problems too. If a Sanguine has chest pain, for example, look to the heart and treat the chest pain as an emergency. If there is a heart trauma, lab tests should examine several enzymes, including CPK, SGOT (a.k.a. AST), and LDH (lactic dehydrogenase). Also check for increased white blood count and increased sedimentation rate. If there is alcohol abuse or overindulgence, check the liver enzymes.

The dietary needs of Sanguine types include high protein. They might tolerate a moderate (but not excessive) amount of alcohol, and they do reasonably well with sugar. Indeed, the Sanguine, within limits, is the only one of the four types that is not bothered by sugar. Still, due to their dietary needs and desires, they may take in an excess of alcohol, sugar, and protein. This, of course, can hurt the heart, which is a muscle, and can produce plaque and arterial sclerosis. If there is plaque, it is appropriate to take enzymes to digest the extra protein. Alcohol and sugar in excess in this type can lead to depression, even though it is not their usual mode.

With regard to nutrition, vitamin C, CoQ$_{10}$, and zinc are essential for the Sanguine, and should be taken with food rather than just a glass of water. Vitamin supplementation is best taken with food in general, and since the Sanguine has the second longest digestive tract, this supplementation is better absorbed with food.

Physiologically, the Sanguine temperament derives from the embryological mesoderm. This gives rise to the skeletal muscle, circulatory and excretory systems, the pulp of the teeth, muscles of the mouth and face, smooth and striated cardiac muscle, connective tissue, cartilage, excretory kidney and ureter, the bladder, and the reproductive system, including testes, vagina, seminal vesicle, breasts, uterus, ovaries, and fallopian tubes. I mention these organs in particular because these are the organs with which Sanguine types might have issues. Major cavities in the body that are derived from the mesoderm occur in the pleura of the lungs, the pericardium, and the peritoneal cavity.

It should be noted that Sanguine types have a tendency to exaggerate medical symptoms. However, if they have an infection and particularly a bacterial infection, it can become severe quickly and can be accompanied by a high fever, and there is often a need for antibiotics or other bactericidal substances to help alleviate the symptoms and eradicate the infection. If you are not a medical doctor, refer them out immediately. The infections are often difficult to treat, so it is best to start treatment early.

Woman with a Classic Sanguine Jawline Seeks Help

A patient with a classic Sanguine jawline came to me with significant neurological deficits. She had been to many different practitioners— neurologists, infectious disease specialists, and regular primary care physicians—to assess what was wrong. She came back with multiple diagnoses. I said to her, "Is there any chance you've been exposed to a tick?" because I was concerned about Lyme disease. She said, "No, I don't think I have Lyme disease. I was tested." I told her I thought she should have that evaluated again because in the case of Lyme disease there are certain special tests that have to be done. You can't just do a regular screening test.

The reason I persisted with Lyme is precisely because the woman was a Sanguine. A Sanguine doesn't normally show up with a primary neurological disturbance as the first part of the body to be affected. It would be more likely that a Sanguine symptom would trace back to the blood. Although the neurological symptoms she presented could have been about a circulatory system compromise, her neurological exam showed that neurological deficit was primary. Her history revealed that she had had signs of an infection. When Sanguine types become infected, that infection can become brutal and vigorous and can be fulminating and move fast.

For this reason I sent her to an infectious disease specialist in Manhattan whom I happened to know as an expert for Lyme. He said to her, "Absolutely. You have Lyme." They started her on intravenous antibiotics immediately and in a couple of months all her neurological symptoms were gone.

So as you can see, taking her morphology into account and knowing that she was a Sanguine and then following the lines of investigation of

infection yielded the proper diagnosis and sped up her recovery. When you
see the morphology, you can see the tendencies and inclinations.

The Lymphatic Profile

When reading the Lymphatic profile, notice that no jawline can be observed because of the overlying flesh. Note that, since the fleshiness of the chin increases in all types with age, most seniors become, at least in part, Lymphatic. When you look at the Lymphatic nature, it seems to jibe with their spiritual and emotional maturity. In the original teaching of morphology it was said not to read the temperament after the age of sixty-five; however, I believe, especially here in America, that people maintain their youth much longer and that the age for reading the temperament can be pushed ahead. The forehead of Lymphatic types is flat, and the back of the head is in the form of an upside down shovel.

Characteristics of the Lymphatic Temperament

- **Prime embryological layer:** Endoderm
- **Season:** Winter
- **Disposition:** The Lymphatic gives support to others.
- **Daily quaternary:** 12:00 a.m.–6:00 a.m. is when the tissue associated with the Lymphatic temperament is nourished and strong.
- **Sleep:** The amount of activity does not affect sleep. The Lymphatic

can sleep at just about any time, and while they may not need it as much as other types, they enjoy sleeping.

• **Skin tone:** White

The Lymphatic type is passive, corporeal (body oriented), and objective (in the sense of being fair-minded), but not indifferent. Also, in the foursquare illustrations we will soon be examining, we will find that the animal that is associated with the Lymphatic temperament is the ox, which is slow, steady, strong, and passive. There are two Lymphatic types: the amorphous, which does not have a well-formed body shape (and so is less active and slower), and the phlegmatic, which has a more organized body shape (and so is more active and balanced).

Since these people live and love to eat, they are always thinking about their next meal. In addition to taking in large amounts of food, they are fully capable of taking in and synthesizing large amounts of information. They are considered the true digestive and absorptive type regarding food, water, and information.

Lymphatic types normally have a pale, whitish complexion and dark brown hair and are typically round or have a round quality, which generally speaks to receptivity and malleability. While a coolness can often be detected in their character, they are not typically callous. They can stay detached. They tend to be the most reliable of all the temperaments and are seen as joyous and passive/receptive with a welcoming spirit. They tend to be good companions—open, accepting, and tolerant— though they are not as sociable as the Sanguine type.

Justice is very important to Lymphatics and because of their objective nature, they make fair and unbiased judges. They also tend to have an excellent, nearly elephant-like memory.

Lymphatic types are homebodies and devotional sorts and are inclined to be religious. They tend to have vivid imaginations, which makes imagery a good healing modality for them, and they are easily able to objectify their experiences. They are not generally interested in the past and are able to easily detach from it.

Lymphatic children need to be allowed to take their time. They require love and privacy. They are to be encouraged in their own interests, solitary as they tend to be.

Lymphatic types are slow, steady, and strong and tend to take their time. They are generally seen as sedentary, and one would not associate activity with them. However, although they find most exercise boring, two forms they enjoy are swimming and walking. Not surprisingly, these people do not like hard physical work. Even so, their forearms have the potential to be very strong, but this requires some form of exercise, which is usually swimming.

Lymphatic types tend to have a lot of endurance. They do their work steadily and evenly, but they are not workaholics. Lymphatic teachers don't typically take breaks when teaching; they can go on and on, which makes it difficult for the other types they are teaching. The Lymphatic student, however, would be quite happy to sit, listen, and read.

With the longest digestive tract of the four temperaments, Lymphatics can digest almost any food, which it may be worth noting is not the best deterrent to overeating. They must be careful not to become addicted to sweets, which for many are generally unhealthy because of the refined sugar, and the Lymphatic type, being derived from the endoderm, which is endocrine, must avoid getting diabetes. Lymphatics are also wise to avoid hot baths and hot showers, since it can weaken them.

Lymphatic problems include fluid retention and the dysfunction of the endocrine glands. Lymphatic types tend to use food to calm themselves, but eating too much food or drinking large amounts of water can cause fluid retention, which can cause these people to become depressed. On the other hand, they tend to do well with coffee, since caffeine is a diuretic and can draw the liquid out of them. Because they are well organized internally and able to absorb and assimilate copious amounts of information, they can use coffee to keep them awake to get their work done quickly. Vitamin B_6 and dandelion root can also lift their mood and dry them out, as they are diuretics as well.

Carbohydrates cause those with a Lymphatic temperament to gain weight, and they should be coached not to eat fats in combination with carbohydrates because they will store one or the other. If a Lymphatic person is overweight, the gallbladder lining may be invaded by fat.

Even though they need to watch their weight, Lymphatics tend to do better when they are ten pounds overweight. When they become too thin, they become lethargic, which weakens their memory. The flesh of their body tends to be the repository of their memory, and their power comes from their fat reserves.

Lymphatic types have to be concerned with the flow of lymph. Sometimes they may have discharge issues, particularly from the sinuses and the vagina.

Because they may be prone to bladder and kidney issues, Lymphatics should include asparagus, watermelon, cucumber, and parsley in their diet. Other helpful nutrients are zinc to support the heart and chlorella or chlorophyll to cleanse the blood.

The embryological layer that the Lymphatic derive from is the endoderm, and as a result Lymphatics often have digestive problems and thyroid dysfunction. Since the endoderm is associated with endocrine issues, diabetes can occur. Additionally, the endoderm gives rise to the lungs, so one with a Lymphatic temperament can be prone to lung dysfunction. Sometimes internal secretory problems can be reflected in the pancreas. The endodermal layer also gives rise to the ducts (where the nodules may become clogged), ductless glands, epithelium of the trachea, bronchi and lungs, lining below the larynx, entire bladder, trigone of the bladder, male and female urethra (except the tip), lining of the pancreas, gallbladder and liver, bile ducts, alimentary canal (except the anus), eustachian tubes, parathyroid, and tonsils.

Lab work studies appropriate for the Lymphatic type are blood sugar, A1C (glycosylated hemoglobin), BUN (blood urea nitrogen), creatinine, thyroid, amylase, lipase, uric acid, and adrenal insufficiency tests. If Lymphatics are diabetic, look toward the pancreas, and if they have chest pain, it is usually digestive in nature.

Bilious, Nervous, Lymphatic— Taking It All with a Grain of Salt

If you have a Saturn front-face (more about planetary influences and front-faces later) Bilious patient who comes in talking about gloom and doom, you might consider it par for the course for them and not necessarily an indication of immediate danger. These types need a long interval between decision and action and might brood while going over all the things in their mind. Considering this may help you understand their behavior. Similarly, when a Nervous type comes in and thinks he or she is dying, of course you consider everything you might do to help the person, but you take their fears with a grain of salt, because the Nervous tend to embellish their health issues and tend to be the most nervous about them. You have the classic Nervous type in Woody Allen.

This means that you have to consider the context in which the person describes his or her issues. For example, Lymphatic types normally do not complain, but if they do, you have got to pay attention, because it could be something quite deep and significant. If a Lymphatic is fleshy and holds everything inside, the issue could be something that is underneath the person's current awareness.

In short, you can see how morphology can help health-care practitioners evaluate the patient's symptoms.

A Short Summation

So far, we have seen some general traits of each of the four temperaments. A summary list of these traits is as follows:

- Bilious types have both physical and mental prowess to execute a task. They are indefatigable, huge collectors of information, and in the extreme can be too bossy or can become despots.

- Nervous types are quick-witted, poetic, creative, and energetic, can tend toward hypochondriasis and nervousness, and can fatigue easily. Their need for adoration, adulation, and acknowledgment can negatively influence their relationships.
- Sanguine types are analytical, jovial, motoric, strong, warrior-like, and able to take risks, and they need to be directed physically. Their potential challenges include being distracted easily, overindulging, and falling prey to addiction.
- Lymphatic types are amiable, independent, religious, passive, sedentary, true absorbers of everything, and in the extreme can overindulge in food. They are generally passive unless provoked. Their potential challenges are that they can be cold and indifferent.

A summary of the digestive characteristics of each temperament is provided in chapter 5 (starting on page 165).

In short, Bilious *know,* Nervous *think,* Sanguine *do,* and Lymphatic *believe.*

A Return to the Number Four

The art and science of face reading is based upon a sacred tradition, which includes the citing of many cases of fours coming together in the creation of man/woman. As discussed in the introduction, we see the number four represented in the four temperaments, the four faces on the four posts of Ezekiel's vision of the chariot, the four Hebrew letters of the tetragrammaton, the four rivers, and the four apostles (sometimes called archangels). Even when we consider the four aspects of the sphinx at Giza, we see that the face represents a man, the tail represents an ox, the body is that of a lion, and the claws are that of an eagle.

While the four temperaments, or the four flows of life force, are in everyone, the Bilious and the Nervous are seen as the intellectual types. The Sanguine and Lymphatic are seen as the body or corporeal types. From another angle, at the outset, we observed the active types as Bilious and Sanguine and the passive types as Nervous and Lymphatic.

ACTIVE OR PASSIVE PHYSIOLOGY WITH INTELLECT OR BODY FOCUS

	Active	Passive
INTELLECT	Bilious	Nervous
BODY	Sanguine	Lymphatic

Remember, all these fours are in a sense the same fours. We shall continue to see them as we continue our journey.

Temperaments and Possible Professions

You now have a good foundation in the basics. In this section we'll consider the inclinations of the temperaments that would most likely lead to fulfillment when choosing a vocation or profession. We begin with the positions that would best suit each of the temperaments in, for example, a company.

- The Bilious would be the boss or the president.
- The Nervous would be the idea person.
- The Sanguine would be the salesperson of the company.
- The Lymphatic would be the top administrator or accountant.

Of course, since we are not pure types, there is much variation in an individual's choice of profession. The following are things to consider:

- The Bilious live from event to event. They have the ability to calculate and execute their plans with their own physicality. They are masterful thinkers and have consistent energy.
- The Nervous tend to need support, and they live from sense impressions. They are very creative and have many innovative ideas but need a staff of mesomorphs to assist them in making their ideas

come to life. We see an excellent example of this in Walt Disney.

- The Sanguine are the truly muscular type. They enjoy physical labor and are analytical. They are easily distracted by anything that comes their way. Due to their physically motoric nature, they tend to move before they think. Even though the Sanguine type is known to be analytical, it is good to remember that movement is still a priority. For best reliability with Sanguines, give action in the moment.

- The Lymphatic are punctual, reliable, and philosophical, and they love to teach. In addition, they like to stay put and only move comfortably within the structure of their work.

While it seems that one particular type may be favorable over another for a certain position, there are so many other aspects of the face that can compensate for weaknesses and balance out abilities, that truly anyone can do anything. However, understanding your nature through face morphology can lead to a happier life as you choose a profession that aligns with your temperament.

Balance and the Law of Reciprocity: How the Masters Read the Face

When looking at the face, one of the elements to evaluate is balance. We look at the right/left symmetry and the three divisions of the front-face, which will be discussed in more detail later. The face can reveal when one is in or out of balance. We know from the law of reciprocity, which says that *the outside reveals the inside and the inside reveals the outside,* that face balance provides vital information about the goings-on inside and outside the person.

Thus, if we see that the face is out of balance, it indicates that there is an imbalance internally. As you learn how to read the face and understand its changes and nuances, you can see where there is an imbalance. And further, you can help yourself, your loved ones, and your patients or clients, if you are a practitioner, to understand what is happening.

> When assessing balance, we look to see whether we are out of balance either in time, which is represented in rhythm and pace, or in space, which is represented in proportion and measure.

Now, I want to underscore and repeat that helping yourself or sharing with others to understand what is happening is simply a denotative typology. As I said earlier: *There is no value judgment here.* We are just observing and noting, not observing and judging. For example, a person can observe that the face of a loved one reveals a change that was not there the day or week before and know that it is possible that such a change might mean there is a movement toward ill health or there is an emotional, mental, or physical issue brewing. When we know how to read the balance, we are able to know what an imbalance represents.

Conversely, we can see that when changes move toward balance, health has improved or an issue has been cleared. When you notice restored symmetry, clarity, or tone, you can tell that an individual is moving toward homeostasis.

As a practitioner observing your patient or client, at any point early on you would inform the person that the study of face morphology is a *reciprocal study,* meaning that what is seen on the outside of the body reflects what is inside as well. The Star of David (see figure 1.3) geometrically depicts a better-known version of this law: "as above, so below." You can see that it consists of a triangle pointing up and a triangle pointing down. "Above, in Heaven, continuing in sameness; Below on Earth."* We can also see from this diagram that there are triangles contained within the star representing the elements

---

*Hermes Trismegistus, *The Corpus Hermeticum,* trans. G. R. S. Mead (Charlotte, N.C.: Information Age Publishing, 2009), 67. Originally from text written circa 100–300 CE.

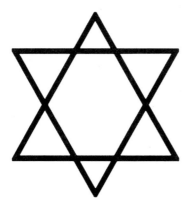

Fig. 1.3. Star of David

fire △, water ▽, air ◬, and earth ⩔ as depicted in the foursquare diagram.*

Also contained within the geometry of the Star of David is a depth of knowledge about the human body and morphology. Hippocrates stated that there are four humors that correlate to the four temperaments.

The following quoted material comes from pages 49–50 of Dennis William Hauck's eloquent description of this topic in his book *Sorcerer's Stone: A Beginner's Guide to Alchemy*.

The "Greek philosopher, considered to be the father of medicine, Hippocrates (400 BCE) . . . viewed the elements as bodily fluids he called 'humors.' In Hippocrates's system, Fire is associated with the choleric humor of yellow bile, which is carried in cholesterol as a by-product of digestion and energy transformation in the body. Aristotle would say the choleric force is hot and dry. Choleric people, therefore, tend to be energetic, active, moving, . . . and enthusiastic."—This is a perfect description of the Bilious temperament. The symbol for fire used by alchemists can be seen in the upward-pointing triangle △ within the Star of David.

---

*The foursquare is central to the study of face morphology. We will look at it in detail in the section titled "Reading the Foursquare" beginning on page 49.

"Water is associated with the phlegmatic humor of phlegm, which represents the clear fluids of the body carried by the lymphatic system and secreted by the mucus membranes. Phlegmatic people are cold and wet in Aristotle's terms and tend to be in touch with their feelings and can be moody and brooding. . . . People in whom the phlegmatic humor is predominant tend to be flowing and flexible, letting their feelings guide them, and oriented toward emotional harmony."—This is a perfect description of the Lymphatic temperament. The symbol for water used by alchemists can be seen in the downward-pointing triangle $\triangledown$ within the Star of David.

"Air is associated with the Sanguine humor of the blood which distributes oxygen throughout the tissues of the body. The word, 'Sanguine,' refers to a ruddy complexion in which the blood flows close to the skin. . . . Sanguine people tend to be very changeable and even flighty, perhaps a little irritable yet basically optimistic, and full of personal integrity. According to Aristotle, such people are hot and wet in their elemental qualities."—This is a perfect description of the Sanguine temperament. The symbol for air, used by alchemists, can be seen in the upward-pointing triangle with a horizontal line through it $\triangle$ within the Star of David.

"Earth is associated with the melancholic humor of black bile, which probably refers to waste products associated with digestion. . . . Melancholic people tend to be apathetic, passive, stubborn, sluggish, and rigid yet practical. . . . The Melancholic humor is dominant in the person who focuses on physical reality and tends to exhibit the qualities of perseverance, inflexibility, realism, and pragmatism. In Aristotle's terms, such people are cool and dry."—This is a perfect description of the Nervous temperament. The symbol for earth used by alchemists can be seen in the downward-pointing triangle with a horizontal line through it $\triangledown$ within the Star of David.

Let me mention here another symbol that recognizes the "as above, so below" principle—the Christian cross (see figure 1.4). Depicted analogically, the cross reveals the vertical reality as the up

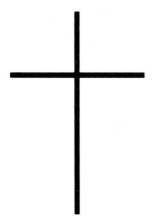

Fig. 1.4. Christian cross

and down line while the horizontal earthly reality is the across line.

Another example of "as above, so below" is seen in the practice of chiropractic. The patient may require stabilization of the cervical spine (neck) that at times cannot be achieved unless stabilization of the lumbar spine (lower back) is accomplished.

"As above, so below" has another application. In our lives, as spiritually aware and awake individuals, we are constantly in a grid where we are trying to keep ourselves in alignment with the Divine or vertical reality, which is the place of no time, while simultaneously being in the horizontal reality, which is time-bound and represents the man-made world. We aspire to be "in the world but not of it," as the expression goes.

While it might be a spiritual practice, balancing and staying in the grid (the crosshairs of the vertical and horizontal reality) is also translated analogically in our body and our face morphology. When looking at the human body, certain correlations between the vertical and horizontal realities can be considered. For instance, the left side of the body is the past, and the right side is the future. And since the horizontal represents the time-bound, man-made reality, it can be helpful to analogically reference the conditions of the manifestation of the person's problem.

> Since the left side of the body represents one's past and the right side of the body represents one's future, if we observe that there are asymmetrical feature changes on one side or the other, it may indicate that the person had a problem in the past or is struggling with the future.

Again, looking at the example of chiropractic, the principles reveal that the impulses carried from Universal Intelligence (God, Spirit) come through the body via the spine in an above-down-in-out movement. When one's spine is in alignment, meaning there are no subluxated vertebrae (fixed in a misaligned position with nerve interference), those impulses flow through the human being vitalizing, energizing, and making healthy the entire body. If, however, the vertebrae move out of alignment into a subluxated position (the bones usually shift right or left), this essentially breaks the vertical flow and locks the person into a time-bound man-made reality. When the spine is properly aligned through the chiropractic adjustment, then there is direct expression from the vertical reality into the person. There is no time, and health is manifested.

The relationship between the mind and the body is another version of "as above, so below." By understanding that there is an intimate relationship between the mind and the body, we can entertain the possibility that when a person has certain thoughts, those thoughts may be reflected in the physical body, and when a person has a physical injury, the physical injury can be reflected in the thoughts. This illustrates the law of reciprocity.*

As mentioned earlier, the law of reciprocity is central to face mor-

---

*In Chinese medicine, the concept of "as above, so below" is referred to as the law of correspondences. This principle is specifically used in acupuncture, where one would use the shoulder to treat the hips, the elbows to treat the knees, the wrists to treat the ankles, and so forth. Keep this in mind when you evaluate your own condition. The "as above, so below" relationship might reveal something to you that might otherwise have gone unnoticed.

phology. It tells us that when changes are made on the face, changes are made inside, and that when changes are made inside, changes are reflected on the face. In essence, the face is a mirror of internal health.

The Profile Angles That Determine Temperaments

Profile angles can help us determine the temperament of an individual. Here is a short guide with illustrations showing how to distinguish one temperament from another by first reading the slope of the forehead and the angle of the jaw in profile and then by adding the shape of the back of the head and the lines of force.

Reading the Forehead and Jaw

The temperament remains somewhat the same during a person's life, and the jaw bones do not grow very much once one has reached his or her adult height, usually at the age of twenty-five, which is when the bones are completely ossified. As noted earlier, with age, the area under the chin can become fleshy and develop a dewlap. Most people become Lymphatic in the later part of life.

The Bilious Temperament

The forehead that is straight up and down or pouched forward is the sign of the Bilious temperament, one of the two active types.

This pouched forehead is accompanied by a jawline that is greater than 90°.

The Nervous Temperament

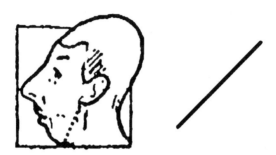

The forehead of the Nervous type is slanted backward (like the Sanguine), but you will notice that it is easy to classify the Nervous temperament by the receding jaw. In fact, it is easy to classify both passive temperaments by the lack of substantial jaws. As you can see in their drawings, the jaws of the Nervous and the Lymphatic temperaments are, so to speak, barely there. The Nervous forehead and jaw both slope backward creating the effect of an arrow-shaped profile.

The Sanguine Temperament

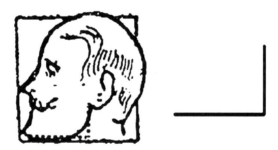

A forehead that angles back is also a sign of the Sanguine temperament, the second active temperament. This forehead angle is accompanied by a jawline that has a 90° angle.

The Lymphatic Temperament

Jaw is obscured by flesh.

The Lymphatic temperament, the second passive type, has a some-what straight forehead, but again it is the "disappearing" jaw that most immediately and effectively announces the passive Lymphatic tempera-ment. Unlike the Nervous type, the jawline of the Lymphatic is typi-cally obscured by flesh or fat.

Reading the Back of the Head

To the slope of the forehead and the angle of the jaw, let us now add the shape of the back of the head, which is different for each temperament as follows:

- **Bilious:** Shaped like a bowling ball
- **Nervous:** Shaped like a soup spoon
- **Sanguine:** Shaped like a spatula (flat back)
- **Lymphatic:** Shaped like a shovel and accompanied by a heavy neck and occipital area

Case of a Most Unusual Head Shape

I was teaching a seminar in New Hampshire, and I noticed that the back of the head of one of the doctors I met was most unusual: there was an asymmetrical bulging of his parieto-occipital area. I was not teaching morphology at the time, I was leading a chiropractic seminar, but when I saw the back of his head, I said to him, "Forgive me, but it looks like you had some cranial injury or something like that," and he revealed to me that he had had a stroke.

I did not know that he had had a stroke specifically, but I knew that something was out of place. The doctor had had a hemorrhagic stroke, so there was an expansion of the cranium on one side, and it showed.

The doctor revealed that he was unable to walk evenly after the traumatic event, and even though he was receiving treatment from a chiropractor, physical therapist, and neurologist, he still had a limp. Since I could see he was a Bilious, I knew his natural head shape should be more bowling ball-like, but instead it was eccentric and bulging. After a specific cranial adjustment that I was able to do right there at the seminar, his head shape changed and his limp disappeared.

If a person has had an injury at any time in their life, that injury is stored in the dural layer of the meninges, which creates a tension in the person's body and affects their posture throughout life. That dural layer protects the brain and inserts itself paravertebrally throughout the spine. That dural tension will cause particular myofascial structures to hold a distinctive posture. For instance, if a person has had a back injury, the dura memorizes that particular injury, and then all the muscles surrounding that area have to adapt. The person might come to complain that one side is weaker than the other, because the memory of the injury is stored right there. In such cases of imbalance, what you want to do, of course, is to create balance. The same situation of cellular memory can be seen if there is an injury to the face or brain. The body makes compensations that may look like distortions that can be easily read. Because the process is physically oriented and can be seen and felt, it can reveal an understanding of a patient's injury. Understanding this, you can see how this simple observation of the back of the head using morphology led me to help this person to restore his normalcy.

Lines of Force

Now that you are familiar with the four temperaments and their profiles, let us look at the lines of force in each of the temperaments as shown in figure 1.5. A line of force is the direction that the energy moves. Notice how the arrows in the figure below demonstrate the direction of force through the part of the face that is dominant in each type.

The Bilious line of force goes upward and forward through the forehead, giving the Bilious that exaggerated forehead and forward movement. The Nervous line of force goes up and backward toward the

Bilious: Line of force moves upward and forward through the forehead.

Nervous: Line of force moves upward and backward through the back of the head.

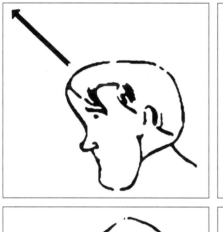
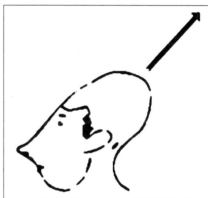

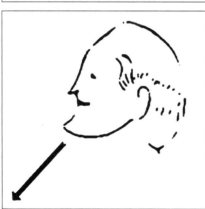
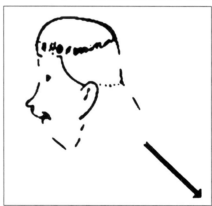

Sanguine: Line of force moves downward and forward through the chin.

Lymphatic: Line of force moves downward and backward through the base of the neck.

Fig. 1.5. Direction of lines of force for each temperament

back of the head, giving the Nervous the bullet-shaped back of the head when seen from profile. The Sanguine line of force goes down and forward through the jaw, so we identify the Sanguine with its strong jaw and forward movement. The Lymphatic line of force goes downward and backward to the back of the base of the head toward the neck. As you proceed in learning about all of the details of the face, you will see how these lines of force influence the interpretation of the features and all of the facial structures.

Reading the
Nose and Temperament

While we will examine the nose in more detail later with other features of the face, this evaluation is to help you establish the temperament.

The nose has two main parts. The first is the bony upper part, which is attached to the root. The root is the place where the nose attaches itself to the forehead, or glabella. The second is the soft cartilaginous part, which begins where the bony part meets the softer lower half to the tip. Each of these parts can be either concave or convex.

The upper bony part of the nose contains the nasal bone. If that part is concave on profile, it is considered a Lymphatic nose. If it is convex, it is a Nervous nose. The convex nose of the Nervous is connected to caring what the world thinks, while the concave nose of the Lymphatic indicates less concern with the world's feelings. The Nervous temperament is very concerned with what the world thinks and tends to find employment based on that. As we noted earlier, Nervous types need adoration and acceptance, which influences their choices and behaviors. Lymphatic types tend to be cooler. Their reaction to the world and what the world thinks of them is less important than it is to the Nervous, which is one of the reasons why, as I noted earlier, Lymphatics tend to be excellent judges. The Nervous or

Lymphatic aspect of the nose is considered a fixity, or having a quality of permanence.

The bottom, cartilaginous part of the nose, or the bulb, is either Bilious or Sanguine. If the bulb is round, it is considered Bilious and tends to signify friendliness and availability to people. It is a wonderful attribute to have and one of the assets of the Bilious type. Karl Malden was well known for that big round tip on his nose. If the bulb is aquiline, it is considered Sanguine. The Sanguine nose tends to accompany a person who is more analytical and less available than the person with the Bilious nose. Sometimes an aquiline nose is pointed, which indicates a quest for learning about humanity. Such people are considered searchers and seekers.

You now have two ways to read the temperaments from the profile— first, the inclination of the forehead with the simultaneous formation of the jaw, and second, the concavity and convexity of the nasal bone along with the shape of the nose tip.

Reading the Foursquare

Now we come to a new way to characterize all the aspects of the four temperaments. The most comprehensive and compact presentation of the four temperaments occurs in what is called the "foursquare" (see figure 1.6 on page 50), in effect a graphic pictorial formulation, which was developed by Gérard Anaclet Vincent Encausse, a.k.a. Papus, and presented in his book *Les Arts Divinatoires* in 1895.

The foursquare is chock-full of information, and in this section we examine the meaning of each element depicted. In addition, you will see that the foursquare symbolically represents key aspects of our humanity. It even gets as specific as the type of exercise that is most beneficial to each temperament and the climate in which each thrives. My aim is to break down this information into small bits to make it easier to understand.

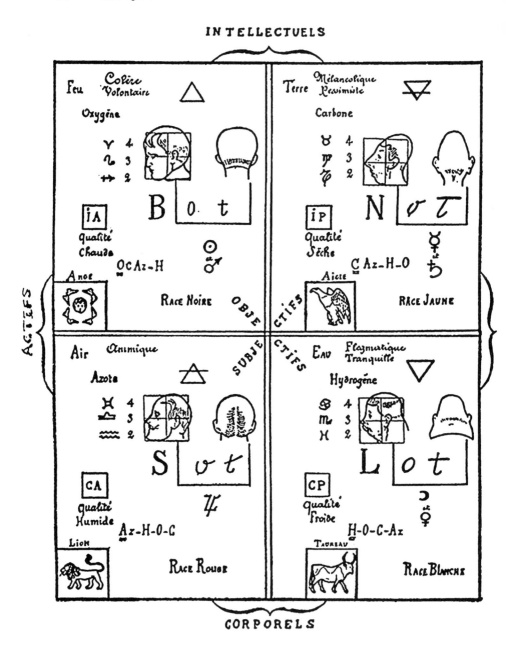

Fig. 1.6. Foursquare
(Created by Gérard Anaclet Vincent Encausse,
from *Les Arts Divinatoires*)

Symbols, Colors, and Shapes
in the Foursquare

In the lower left corner of each square you can see the creature that is associated with one of the four temperaments. Starting with the square in the upper left, you see the man (or angel) that is associated with Bilious; in the upper right square you see the Eagle that is associated with Nervous; in the lower left square you see the lion that is associated with Sanguine; and in the lower right square you see the ox that is associated with Lymphatic.

Now if you look at the center of each square, you will see a picture of the temperament's profile. Starting again with the upper left square, the reverse question mark-shaped profile is associated with Bilious. In the upper right square, the arrow-shaped profile is associated with Nervous. In the lower left square the sloped-back forehead and strong angular-jaw profile is associated with Sanguine. In the lower right square the big neck with no obvious jaw profile is associated with Lymphatic.

Taking the same route, if we look at the upper left and upper right corners of each square, we see the name and symbol, respectively, of an element.

- *Feu* (fire) and the right-side-up triangle are associated with Bilious.
- *Terre* (earth) and the upside-down triangle with a line drawn across it are associated with Nervous.
- Air and the right-side-up triangle with the line across it are associated with Sanguine.
- *Eau* (water) and the upside-down triangle are associated with Lymphatic.

On the bottom right corner of each square, you can see the name of a color. Again, following the same path you see *noire* (black) for Bilious, *jaune* (yellow) for Nervous, *rouge* (red) for Sanguine, and *blanche* (white) for Lymphatic.

Now if you look to the right of the center portrait of the profile, you see a picture of the back of each temperament's head. The shapes resemble a bowling ball for Bilious, a soup spoon for Nervous, a spatula for Sanguine, and a shovel that is narrow at the top and wider at the bottom for Lymphatic.

As you look at the foursquare, notice that the words *objectifs* (objectives) and *subjectifs* (subjectives) crisscross at the center of the square. The "objective" opposites are Bilious and Lymphatic, while the "subjective" opposites are Sanguine and Nervous.

You will also note that *passifs* (passives) and *actifs* (actives) are written outside the two vertical edges of the foursquare. "Passive," or receptive, represents Nervous and Lymphatic, while "active" represents Sanguine and Bilious.

In the lower left area of each quadrant, you will see two words under a square containing two letters. IA means "intellective active," IP means "intellective passive," CA means "corporeal active," and CP means "corporeal passive." Below these notations there is a description of the quality of climate native to each temperament. Note that each type, then, requires its opposite living environment to provide balance.

- *Qualité chaude* (hot quality): Bilious is hot and also dry and does best in a cold, wet environment.
- *Qualité sèche* (dry quality): Nervous is dry and also cold and does best in a wet, hot environment.
- *Qualité humide* (wet quality): Sanguine is wet and also hot and does best in a dry, cold environment.
- *Qualité froide* (cold quality): Lymphatic is cold and also wet and does best in a hot, dry environment.

In the upper left corner of each quadrant, we also see the atomic element that is associated with and most important for each temperament as follows: *oxygène* (oxygen) for Bilious, *carbone* (carbon) for Nervous, *azote* (nitrogen) for Sanguine, and *hydrogène* (hydrogen) for Lymphatic.

In the lower center area of each quadrant you will notice a row of elements listed by their symbols from the periodic table of elements. Most include dashes separating them although Bilious and Nervous seem to be missing some. For example, in Bilious you see "OCAz-H," (or O-C-Az-H), standing for oxygen, carbon, nitrogen, and hydrogen, respectively, and in Nervous you see "C Az-H-O" (or C-Az-H-O). Each temperament has the same four essential elements in a different order, as you will see in the numbered lists later in this section. The order indicates the temperament's primary, secondary, tertiary, and quaternary elemental needs, with the primary element indicated by the first letter in each row (O in Bilious, C in Nervous, and so forth).

Knowing the associated atomic elements gives us information about the typology of each of the four temperaments. The elements point to dietary and respiratory intake, exercise requirements, activity or passivity needs, the ideal kind of living environment, and whether emphasis is on the body or the intellect.

The following list identifies how the primary element of each temperament relates to food selection:

- Bilious gets oxygen from all types of food since they are omnivores.
- Sanguine gets nitrogen mainly from meat protein.
- Nervous gets carbon from grains and vegetables.
- Lymphatic gets hydrogen from modest water intake.

Drawing on the same four elements, the next four lists identify major characteristics that flow from the order of these elements.

Bilious Elements

1. Oxygen
2. Carbon
3. Nitrogen
4. Hydrogen

Because oxygen is their primary element, these individuals make great marathon runners.

Nervous Elements

1. Carbon
2. Nitrogen
3. Hydrogen
4. Oxygen

These people make great dancers and fencers. Their breathing is light and shallow, and they make a lot of CO_2. However, because they primarily have short spurts of energy, they do not do anything that is rigorous.

Sanguine Elements

1. Nitrogen
2. Hydrogen
3. Oxygen
4. Carbon

Sanguine types are muscle builders. They do well with heavy work and weight lifting.

Lymphatic Elements

1. Hydrogen
2. Oxygen
3. Carbon
4. Nitrogen

These individuals love the water and make good swimmers. They have endurance but are not associated with heavy physical activity. They are also contemplative and passive. Their objectivity makes them great judges.

In the lower-right area of each quadrant you see planetary symbols: Sun and Mars for Bilious, Mercury and Saturn for Nervous, Jupiter for Sanguine, and Moon and Venus for Lymphatic. Note that these planets relate to the astrological symbols (see below) and do not correspond to the planetary front-faces we will be discussing later.

To the left of the profile within each quadrant you will see astrological symbols. These symbols represent the astrological signs of the elements that correspond to each temperament.

* Aries, Leo, and Sagittarius represent fire for Bilious.
* Taurus, Virgo, and Capricorn represent earth for Nervous.
* Gemini, Libra, and Aquarius represent air for Sanguine.
* Cancer, Scorpio, and Pisces represent water for Lymphatic.

In the middle of each quadrant, on the right below the images of the backs of the heads, there are incomplete rectangles with two letters, *o* and *t*. These represent handwriting characteristics of each of the temperaments.

As we can see, the foursquare contains much information. This pictorial representation of the temperaments is a wonderful, handy reference.

Quiz:
Identifying the Four Temperaments

This is a little test in identifying the temperaments through profile observations. Take a look at the drawings of archetypal temperaments below and, in the blanks beside them, write down the temperament that matches each profile. Answers follow the images.

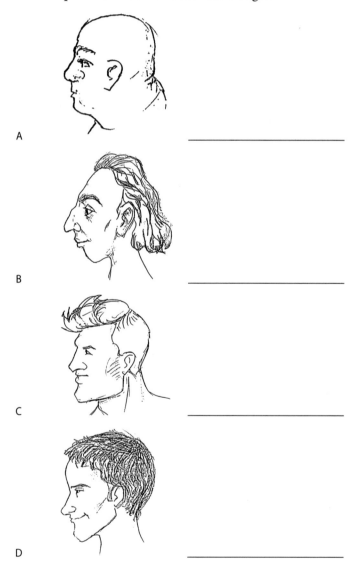

A   _____

B   _____

C   _____

D   _____

Answers—A: Lymphatic; B: Nervous; C: Sanguine; D: Bilious

2
Reading the Front-Face

In this section we will look at the shape of the front of the face, referred to as the "front-face," associated with each temperament and notice how the shape tempers or modifies the profile we examined in the previous section. Our focus there was on how to read the angle of the forehead, the angle of the jaw, the shapes of the back of the head, and the profile of the nose. In this chapter, we concentrate on how to read the front-face. While the profile reveals the temperament, the front-face reveals the personality.

Before continuing, let me say that I believe face reading is a God-given intuitive gift, albeit often best guided when there is a structure of knowledge that it can flow through. Knowing this, one should not try to intellectualize the gift while reading a face. Trust your heart, and the knowledge you are acquiring, and the face will reveal much to you.

In my case, I was comforted to learn about face reading in this didactic way and to have it confirm feelings and thoughts that I had had about myself and loved ones. Say you look in the mirror and you say, "Oh my goodness there is a pimple right there on the tip of my nose." Maybe you used to think to yourself, "Could it be the chocolate I ate?" But now, with this knowledge of face morphology, you know that that pimple could relate to some biological event in your body. Later in the book, you will learn about the individual features and how the location of as simple a thing as a pimple on the tip of the nose could represent a heart dysfunction . . . or just chocolate. This is the way you begin to read the many kinds of facial glyphs.

Now let us see what we can learn about and from front-faces.

Big Face and Little Face

As you look at front-faces, begin to distinguish the big face and the little face (see figure 2.1). The big face is the outer face, or frame. The little face is the space of the sensory receptors—the eyes, nose, and mouth. At the same time, each part of the face here, big and little, can be seen as a hologram that speaks to the whole person's nature.

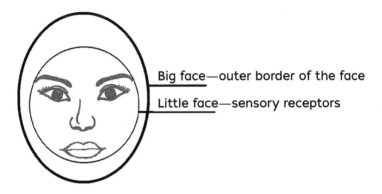

Big face—outer border of the face

Little face—sensory receptors

Fig. 2.1. Big face, little face

When observing the relationship between the big face and the little face, we often see that it reflects a person's capacity to be open to the world. For example, if you see large receptors on the little face with a small big face (see figure 2.2), then it is possible that the person can be easily sensorially and physically overwhelmed because too much comes in at once. The reverse is similarly true. If one has a large big face and a small little face (small, closely positioned receptors) (see figure 2.3), it might be difficult to get through to that person. This would be someone for whom you might need to speak louder, make especially large gestures, or have some other method of stimulation to get them to see your point.

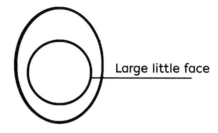

Large little face

Fig. 2.2. Large little face, small big face

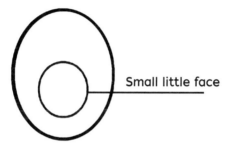

Small little face

Fig. 2.3. Large big face, small little face

An Adult Child Who Won't Listen

I had a mother come in recently with an adult child (who independently had come to me for help many times before). She said, "Is there anything you could say to my son? He just won't listen." I looked at her and in front of her son I unfortunately had to say, "No." I said, "I've known him for many, many years. He almost never listens. It's in his face not to. He has a huge big face and small receptors, so he doesn't hear what's being said. He doesn't take it in. He's only in his own place." And she said, "That's right." With this revelation, the parent chose not to be so frustrated and found different ways to communicate with her son without the expectation of him getting it in the typical way.

As for small little face receptors in a small big face, this tends to denote an introverted person who is shy and weak. The life of such people tends to be mostly about their own personhood. They are not interested in allowing people in from the outside.

The relationship of big face and little face applies to young children too. Indeed, when dealing with children, your own children in particular, observing the relationship of the big face and the little face is an easy, quick technique to help you know how to communicate in a safe and loving way.

Autistic Kids with Big Receptors

I take care of a lot of autistic spectrum kids, and when they have a small face with big sensory receptors, I try to cue in the mothers to be careful with overstimulation. They confirm my concern by agreeing that, yes, their children can't go to a movie or a concert because it's overwhelming for them. And while this might be true for most spectrum individuals, those with large receptors can experience these activities as unbearable.

A Woman with Big Receptors

A new patient came to my office. She was seventy-eight years old and very intelligent. She had large receptors and a relatively small big face. Her daughter brought her in and asked if I would do a morphological reading. I agreed and asked the patient if she wanted it. I could tell she was a little guarded. I didn't want to overwhelm her in any way, so I just explained the part about the big face and the little face and that she had large receptors. I explained that it would be my impression that she could be overwhelmed easily by loud sounds or big crowds and she immediately agreed. "Absolutely!" she said.

She said that she was a schoolteacher and that she was fine in the classroom and was wonderful with one or two people. But if she was with a large group of people or at a party, she could not handle it. She pulled herself out of the situation. Loud noises and a cacophony of ambient sounds also disturbed her.

The woman spoke openly because she felt acknowledged by my comment and was able to give herself permission to go into more intimate details about her life that her daughter had not heard before. When you understand even a little bit about the morphology of a person, the person can feel acknowledged—like you "get them," and they get that you get them. When truth is spoken without judgment, people are very open. As in this case, the result can be a heartwarming situation.

The recommendation for people in situations where they feel overwhelmed is to try to make their receptors smaller. For instance, they can squint their eyes or pull in their lips. (Another technique unrelated to the face is to hide their thumbs inside their fists.) Any of these gestures can give the person a little bit of a filter.

In short, as I hope these examples suggest, just by observing the relationship between the big face and the little face in one glance, you can understand a person's life with regard to their general relationship to the world.

Balance

At the risk of being repetitious, let me note again that when you are a morphologist, and you are looking at a person's face, you are not trying to change the person. Your aim, as always, is to share the information you glean from the face with that person so that she can use it beneficially. You are alerting her to her imbalances. In many cases you are *confirming* imbalances that the individual has felt in her life—and as a practitioner you can respond to a client's requests to make a change in herself, showing her how to change her morphology for better adaptation.

It is a good practice for anyone to look in the mirror and evaluate balance in his or her own face. If one lives with others, visual evaluation can help a person see whether the faces of those they live with are balanced as well. It is true that we know intuitively when someone is sad or happy. However, when you become familiar with the features in your own face, it becomes easier to read clues in the faces of other people and see if something might be going awry.

Face morphology is very analytical, but there is also a huge intuitive aspect to it. This means that you have, within you, the ability to see right away any aspect of the face that stands out on a person. For example, once you are familiar with assessing big face and little face, you might notice the size of the nose or the size of the eyes or the prominence of the ears. With this impression, you get an idea, or a picture, about the way that person moves through his life.

Intuition about the Nose of a Little Boy

A little boy came into my office. I'd seen him before, but I noticed for the first time that his nose was highly aquiline (straight) and the shape of his nostrils (long and narrow) indicated a high degree of intelligence. But there was something about his features that made the nose stand out to me.

Because he was considered to be on the autism spectrum, I asked the mother how he was with smells. She said he was hypersensitive to smells, and more than that, he was hypersensitive to sounds as well. Multiple senses can be hyperactive in autistic people. What was revealed morphologically was the nose, which clued me in to the sensory overload.

Because I use variations of applied kinesiology* in my practice, I used a muscle test to get information about certain areas of his brain, and what kept coming up was "olfactory bulb," which is a neural structure involved in the sense of smell. I find this frequently on children who are on the autism spectrum. And since the olfactory bulb is very close to the limbic system, and the limbic system is associated with emotional response, this can become key to helping these children. We all know that engaging certain senses can trigger an emotional response.

What was encouraging to me in this case was that the kinesiological finding, his clinical correlation of having olfactory hypersensitivity, and being on the autism spectrum, in connection with the anatomical proximity of the olfactory bulb to the limbic system, were all pointing to something.

---

*Applied kinesiology was developed from traditional kinesiology by Dr. George Goodheart in 1964. It is a system of both manual muscle testing and therapy based on the observation that organ dysfunction is reflected in the body as muscle weakness.

The intention then was to see if we could utilize his sense of smell to help him modulate his emotions. I recommended essential oils that the mother could use when he was having his difficulties.

When his mother brought him in for that particular visit, she said he was beside himself. We were not sure what the cause was, perhaps the lunar eclipse or exposure to toxic dye or something else. Many times these children can have an overwhelming experience referable to the environment, and it sets them off. After observing his nose and the olfactory center correlation, I recommended the use of salt baths to detoxify his body. This lessening of the toxic load would reduce the sensory overactivity. On subsequent visits his mother thanked me, as employing the essential oils and bath salts gave her something effective to do when she couldn't, as happened in the past, calm him down.

It bears mentioning that the intuitive aspect of face reading played a key role in my ability to help this child. Simply observing this child's nose opened up an avenue of inquiry that I felt would not only help him but many others, and I am now exploring how to work with these kids via the pathway of the nose. Morphological practice opens up the intuitive channel.

Remember, morphology is an objective assessment used to help one achieve balance, not to change oneself into something different. So, for example, if you are a Lymphatic, you would not try to change yourself into a Bilious. Similarly, when interacting with any other temperament, you would try to help individuals find balance within their own temperament. If you are a clinical practitioner, when you are interested in sharing your findings with your patients or clients, you would look at their faces for symmetrical balance and simply seek to share what you observe.

Measurements of the Face

In this text we are not going to use the quantitative tape measure approach that the French have applied in their very extensive examination and interpretation of the distances between different features on the face. However, there are some physical phenomena that can be seen without pulling out a tape measure. For example, let's look again at the face from the side. This time, instead of looking for indicators of temperament, we are simply looking at relationships of proportion. When viewing the face from the side with this intention, you can *visually* measure the distance between the nose and the tragus, which is the out-pouching of the cartilage on the part of the ear closest to the cheek (see figure 2.4). The longer the distance between the nose and the

Short distance from
tip of nose to tragus

Long distance from
tip of nose to tragus

Fig. 2.4. Tragus to nose distance, short and long

tragus, the more active motorically a person is. The shorter the distance, the less active motorically a person is.

The distance between the tragus and the antitragus, called the intertragus space (see figure 2.5), can also indicate how talkative one is. As you will discover, the larger the distance, the more talkative a person will be, the shorter the distance, the less talkative.

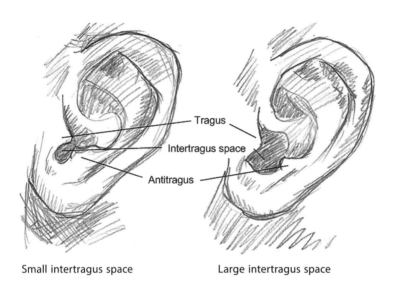

Small intertragus space   Large intertragus space

Fig. 2.5. Small and large intertragus space

Dividing the Face into Three Zones

Now we take a more general look at the front-face, which we can divide into three zones (see figure 2.6 on page 66):

1. The top, which goes from the hairline to the eyebrow, is considered the intellectual zone.
2. The middle, which goes from the eyebrow to the bottom of the nose, is the emotional and social zone.
3. The lower, which goes from the bottom of the nose to the bottom of the chin, is considered the material or instinctual zone.

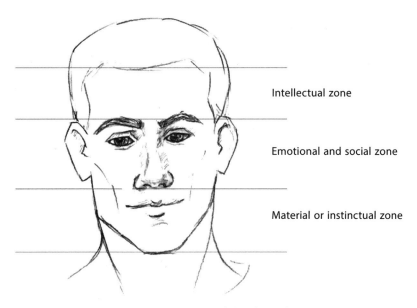

Intellectual zone

Emotional and social zone

Material or instinctual zone

Fig. 2.6. The zones of the front-face

There should be a certain balance of all these three zones, but they are not of equal size (see figure 2.7). When you see that any one of these zones is predominant, you instinctively receive a quick assessment of the person's proclivity in life. For instance, if you see a large forehead in the intellectual zone, you know the person is going to be involved in intellectual pursuits for most of his life, whereas if you see someone with a very large emotional zone, you know she is preoccupied with feelings and what is happening in her social life. And if you see a large lower zone, that person is looking for the acquisition of funds and concrete material gains. People with large lower zones also like to be constructors, builders, and contractors. They know how to take raw materials and turn them into something of value. They may be very sharp and astute in the physical world.

Intellectual Zone in a Child

A child was brought to me many years ago. The mother was concerned that he would never fit in the world because he was developmentally delayed. I kept affirming that he was a genius. You could see in his face

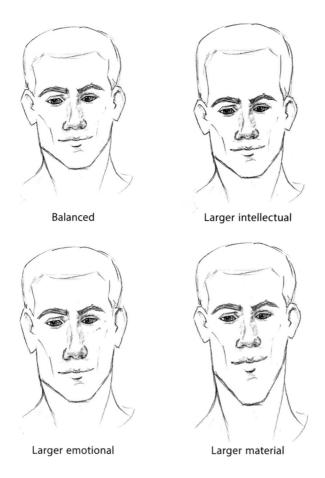

Balanced   Larger intellectual

Larger emotional   Larger material

Fig. 2.7. Examples of different size zones of the front-face

that his intellectual zone was huge. He had the morphology of a very bright, intelligent person, but his facies—expressions that are typical of a particular condition—made him look like someone who was slow or mentally delayed. His mouth was open, and he had very slow, affected speech. I said to the mother, I'm certain that he is going to reveal himself with time. He doesn't have skills yet to do this. He has motor deficiency, but he doesn't have mental deficiency.

Now he is older, and the mother told me that he is a math savant. He has a memory for dates and can absolutely tell you what happened on May 5, 1992, or any other random date. He is extremely savvy with the computer, and he has an extraordinary memory. He is only in his teens now, but certainly there will be a way to funnel that talent into something that he can use in life.

I'd known the child for years, and I kept sticking to my guns, and now the proof is out. It is interesting to know that you can accurately read the morphology even when the person is very young.

A critical aspect of these facial zones is that each one can be balanced by a different part of the body. The intellectual zone is correlated to the chest, the emotional zone is correlated to the upper abdomen, and the concrete (or material) zone is correlated to the lower abdomen. By correlated, I mean that these three parts of the face can reflect conditions in certain various parts of the body.

Thus, if there is a color change or pimples or other marks in any of the zones, you would want to look at the correlating zone of the body for any kind of distress. For example, blemishes, moles, scars, or discolorations in the emotional zone—between the bottom of the nose and the eyebrows—might hint that an investigation should be made for whether an ulcer, hiatal hernia, or gallbladder distress are correlating symptoms in the upper abdomen. Or if someone has many pimples on the lower chin, you might want to look at the lower abdomen for bowel distress, uterine disorders, or prostate problems. And, to extend this last example, if the individual also has a very large material zone—bottom of the nose to bottom of the chin—you want to include that assessment when you look at their bowel habits, their evacuation of the large intestine, and their prostate, uterus, or ovaries.

Now imagine that a person has a very large intellectual zone but does not have a large chest. You might check for mental instability, or mental imbalance, or, in the extreme, mental illness.

In keeping with this discernment, if we see someone with a very large emotional zone, we would question the integrity of the stomach, small intestine, liver, or gallbladder. This may correlate to them experiencing phobias or feelings of anger or vulnerability. In Traditional

Chinese Medicine, or TCM, which we will discuss in a later section, emotional associations with organs have been established for five thousand years. From these correlations, we know that when the stomach is involved, one may experience phobia. If the small intestine is involved, one may experience feelings of vulnerability. If the liver is involved, one may experience anger. If the gallbladder is involved, it could be resentment.

The basic point is this: the balance of the areas in the body will be reflected in the balance of the areas of the face.

Face Color and the Three Zones

There is much to be seen in a face, and when we consider color, shape, skin tone, projections, indentations, concavities, convexities, and moles, we must note where they are located. Each of these components enhances the morphology by giving a nuance to the area in which it is contained. Let us first consider skin tone and color changes.

I mentioned earlier that the Bilious skin tone is brown, the Nervous skin tone is yellow, the Sanguine skin tone is red, and the Lymphatic skin tone is white. Imagine now that you are looking at a forehead, and it is beet red. This could tell you many things. The red color of Sanguine with its location in the intellectual zone of the face could clue you in that there is a Sanguine nature in the intellective process. Knowing the Sanguine to be analytical, you may query what this person had been thinking over the past several weeks.

Imagine now that you see a yellow color in the emotional zone (assuming jaundice has been ruled out). You may wonder if the person had had any fearful or worried feelings in the past several weeks.

Now let's say that you see a brown color in the material zone. You may wonder what this person was trying to conquer or what constructive plan was afoot.

So you can see that the elements of shape, size, and color offer distinctions when applied to the different morphological parts of the face.

Front-Face Shape:
The Greek Tradition and the
Four Temperaments

In the tradition of the Greek god typology (the Romans had a similar one), the front-face shapes correlate to the quality of each godhead as can be seen in figure 2.8. (Note that in the sections below, the god and planetary names are reversed from their order in the figure to emphasize the planet rather than the god.)

Each of the four temperaments has two or more corresponding front-face shapes. The front-faces that are associated with a temperament have the quality of that temperament.

The Bilious temperament has three front-faces: Earth/Eos, which is a square shape; Saturn/Chronos, which is a trapezoid shape; and Uranus, which is a long trapezoid shape.

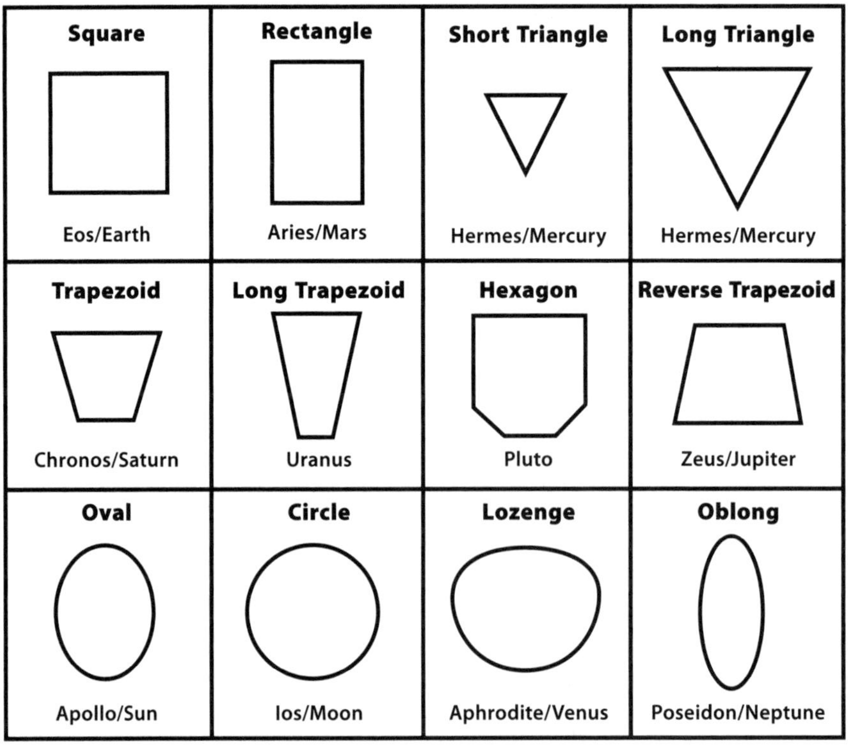

Square	Rectangle	Short Triangle	Long Triangle
Eos/Earth	Aries/Mars	Hermes/Mercury	Hermes/Mercury
Trapezoid	**Long Trapezoid**	**Hexagon**	**Reverse Trapezoid**
Chronos/Saturn	Uranus	Pluto	Zeus/Jupiter
Oval	**Circle**	**Lozenge**	**Oblong**
Apollo/Sun	Ios/Moon	Aphrodite/Venus	Poseidon/Neptune

Fig. 2.8. Front-face shapes in the Greek tradition

The Nervous temperament has two front-faces: short Mercury/ Hermes, which is a short triangular shape, and long Mercury/Hermes, which is a long triangular shape.

The Sanguine temperament has four front-faces: Pluto, which is a hexagon; Mars/Aries, which is a rectangle; Sun/Apollo, which is an oval egg shape; and Venus/Aphrodite, which is a lozenge heart shape.

The Lymphatic temperament has three front-faces: Moon/Ios, which is a circular shape; Jupiter/Zeus, which is a reverse trapezoid shape; and Neptune/Poseidon, which is an oblong capsule shape.

Now, let us look at these faces in more detail. For your convenience, next to each face below is a graphic taken from figure 2.8 on page 70. The drawings might remind you of someone you know. They are not exact diagrams of the planetary shapes; they represent what real people might look like.

Bilious's Three Front-Faces
Saturn/Chronos

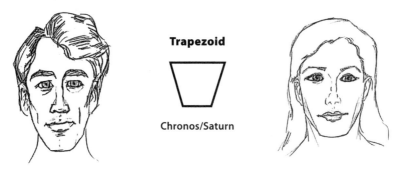

Fig. 2.9. Male and female Saturn/Chronos with corresponding trapezoid shape

Saturn is an elongated trapezoid, wider at the top with a squared-off chin (see figure 2.9, above). Humphrey Bogart, Carole King, and James Dean are all Saturn types. Interestingly, we will see that the Bilious who have a Saturn-type face can have more bone problems than other Bilious types and need calcium, vitamin A, and oxygen. Those with osteoarthritis may need supplementation with phosphorus.

Saturn types tend to be logical, so if you are trying to win an argument with one, do not attack on moral grounds, only on rational. They are also inclined to ponder and ruminate and often have difficulty with imagery as they need more time to process it. They are the most contemplative type and therefore tend to take a long time between thought and action. This gap between thought and action is often mistakenly interpreted as procrastination, an uninformed designation on the part of the observer.

Saturn activities tend to be associated with time, and they are often connected to the past. Another example of a Saturn type is Sigmund Freud, a man for whom therapy was essentially past-oriented. Unfortunately, since anyone who frequently contemplates the past can get morose or depressed, Saturn people show these tendencies when their contemplative, reflective focus becomes stuck in the past.

Saturn types are great long-distance runners and are considered to be the most sexual type of all the front-faces. They can be natural bosses but must be careful not to take their authority to the point of dictatorship.

Earth/Eos

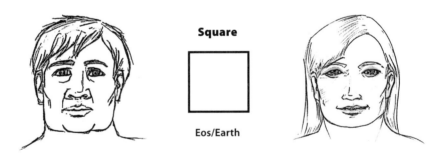

Square

Eos/Earth

Fig. 2.10. Male and female Earth/Eos with
corresponding square shape

Earth is a square-shaped front-face (see figure 2.10, above). For a good example of this geometry, find a picture of Jimmy Cagney as the character he played in the movie *Yankee Doodle Dandy.* People with this front-face are intelligent, concrete, practical, logical, and emotionally strong, and they can be healers. In relationships they can be possessive. They are also muscular and physical and are comfortable in a squatting position where they can stay close to the earth. These types also tend to do very well with money, which is all to their good because they feel they need to have money and *things.* While the following is not a rule, it is a good possibility: if the Earth type has an upturned nose, which in morphology we call a pugnacious nose, they might enjoy fisticuffs.

Uranus

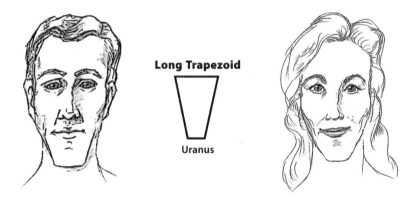

Fig. 2.11. Male and female Uranus with corresponding long trapezoid shape

A long trapezoid (an elongated Saturn) front-face shape is known as Uranus (see figure 2.11, above), and it is the least common front-face. Uranus types are far-reaching thinkers, ahead of their time. When you spot a Uranus person, you might take note that he is likely to influence society. One Uranus we have seen in our history is Edward R. Murrow (see figure 2.12 on page 74), who was considered a visionary in his time. This is interesting because people with a long trapezoid tend to be visionary in their thoughts, though they can exaggerate. The Bilious

Fig. 2.12. Edward R. Murrow
(In the film *The Challenge of Ideas,* 1961)

Uranus type is extremely perseverant, and they can go even deeper than the Bilious Saturn type. They are great researchers, they tend to be bosses, and can be considered know-it-alls. They are creative and attentive but tend to dress without attention to color coordination. They tend to be fine musicians.

Nervous's Two Front-Faces

Mercury and Long Mercury/Hermes

Both the long and short Mercury shapes of the Nervous temperament are triangles with the point at the chin (see figure 2.13, on the facing page), and they share similar qualities. Mercury types are nimble and acrobatic as well as quick-minded and highly communicative. Mercury is associated with the god Hermes who is synonymous with speed. He had wings on his heels. Mercury types can be tricksters. They have a reputation for being elusive, impractical, very sensitive, high-strung, and unpunctual and need the six *A*'s: attention, admiration, adulation,

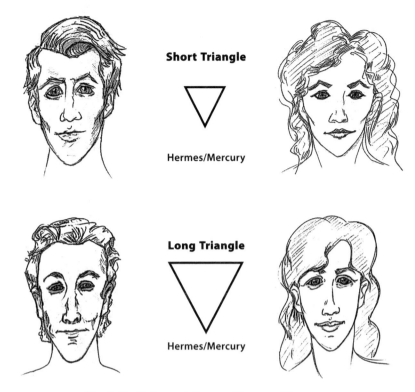

Short Triangle

Hermes/Mercury

Long Triangle

Hermes/Mercury

Fig. 2.13. Male and female Mercury/Hermes, short (top) and long (bottom), and their corresponding triangle shapes

applause, acclaim, and acceptance. They are not interested in the past. Woody Allen is a good example of this type. Although the Mercury Nervous types complain the most, they tend to live the longest. These people can be healers but are mostly associated with being performers. An example of a long Mercury face can be seen in Fred Astaire and a short Mercury face can be found on Michael Jackson and a young Joan Rivers. While Mercury types enjoy the limelight, they need to take breaks during activities.

You often find Mercury people asking others to handle their money. This is because mercury is quicksilver and reflects how money can slip through the fingers fast. Mercury types will lose money if they have to hold it themselves.

Sanguine's Four Front-Faces
Mars/Aries

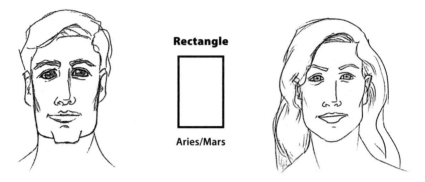

Fig. 2.14. Male and female Mars/Aries with
corresponding rectangle shape

The Mars shaped face is clearly a rectangle (see figure 2.14, above). It is seen in Ronald Reagan, Tom Cruise, Paul Newman, and Farrah Fawcett. The eyes of the Sanguine Mars are generally pale blue, sometimes considered ice blue, which is associated with a coolness and detachment. Because of this quality, coupled with the analytical nature they get from Sanguine, they can be excellent in business. They can get things done without being influenced by emotion.

In their social life, Mars can be gregarious and extroverted, and they can have a short attention span, which makes them easily bored. It can be difficult for them to make long-term plans.

People with the rectangular Mars shape tend to be fickle, impetuous, hot-tempered, and warlike. If the hair is red, they are notorious for being feisty, and if triggered they can be quick-tempered. They tend to be army officers of which one example is General Patton. The Mars loves the military, and, often analogized with Aries the god of war, they tend to make the greatest warriors.

In terms of health, their adrenals get stressed, which can be helped with vitamin C, and they tend toward genital trouble, which can be helped with vitamin E. Due to their Sanguine nature they tend to be muscular.

Pluto

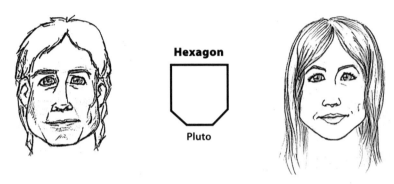

Fig. 2.15. Male and female Pluto with corresponding hexagon shape

The Pluto shape (see figure 2.15, above) is a hexagon and is considered the rarest of the Sanguines. It's thought to be a modified Mars shape. The distinctive characteristic of Pluto is the deep, dark, violet blue piercing eye color as contrasted with the light blue eyes of Mars. The Pluto type likes money, tends to be able to earn it easily, and has an uncanny ability to handle money. In business Plato individuals can be a little amoral. Unlike the Mars shape, they are incredibly loyal and great caregivers. Like other Sanguines, the Pluto types tend to be prone to muscle, joint, and cardiovascular stress along with adrenal weakness and sexual glandular problems. They are bodily oriented. They need to run and have their muscles worked on, and they love the gym. Plutos are generally highly optimistic, social, very organized, caring, and extremely loyal. Good examples of the Pluto shape are Ginger Rogers and Brad Pitt.

Venus/Aphrodite

Venus has a lozenge-shaped, sometimes described as a heart-shaped, face (see figure 2.16, on the next page). Those with a Venus front-face shape

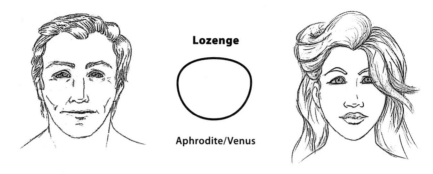

Fig. 2.16. Male and female Venus/Aphrodite with
corresponding lozenge shape

love home and family life. They are very independent and tend to be sought after romantically. Most typically, Venus types love to be flattered. Venuses thrive on the relationships they have with their family, their loved ones, and also with beautiful things. When all of those are in order, they are said to be "aesthetically correct." They make excellent designers because they love to make beautiful decor.

Venus types are typically spunky and resourceful, are often considered clever, and tend to chatter. It is not uncommon for them to be able to move easily from mate to mate. You can see an example of this in Elizabeth Taylor. Even so, Venus types need to have family. *Love* is their byword. They have thick wavy auburn hair with very dark clear blue eyes. The distinctive features that characterize the female Venus are sloping shoulders, breast nipples that fall to the level of the elbow crease, and a mole on the cheek above the lateral lip.

The Sanguine Venus type tends to be sexual. They relinquish relationships easily, without concern, because they know a new relationship is on the heels of the last one. Venuses pick up social causes and tend to be quite talkative. Venuses are consolatory and try to avoid confrontation. They always want everything to go smoothly. Many Venus types are drawn to the entertainment business.

Venus people are primarily mesoderms and when they work out, they build muscle easily. Robert Taylor is a good example. They may be prone to reproductive and muscle problems, and they like and need massage.

Venus

I have a patient who has a beautiful Venus-shaped face. She had raised four children and while she was already educated she was looking for something new to do as an empty nester. She became a feng shui master and an interior designer, which were choices that matched the Venus type, who wants beauty and loves beautiful things.

Sun/Apollo

Oval

Apollo/Sun

Fig. 2.17. Male and female Sun/Apollo with corresponding oval shape

The fourth Sanguine front-face shape is the Sun, an oval, like an upturned egg (see figure 2.17, above) and can be seen in John Glenn, Chuck Yeager, Yul Brynner, the young Dwight D. Eisenhower, and Kate Middleton. Sun types have a high, domed forehead and are considered headstrong, commanding, serious, and naturally detached. They are also idealistic and athletic and generally have a goal, ambition, or ideal that they hold on to and work toward fulfilling for their entire life.

Sun types tend to be choosy, and they know a lot of things before most people. They are natural leaders. Being charismatic, they attract many people to themselves and are very willing to share their ideas and possessions. They do not need more than one or two close friends, but they are extremely sociable. Pathognomonic traits for Sun are green eyes with occasional gold flecks and square shoulders. Scandinavian Suns have blue eyes.

Sun Face over Time

I had not seen one of my patients in a long while. When he came in, he looked the same except that he no longer had hair on his head. You could see where the hairline was, and his Sun face could still be read. Sun types carry the same set of ideals, ideas, beliefs, thoughts, and principles throughout their lives, and it was interesting to me that even though I had not seen him in probably twenty years, these aspects hadn't changed. It's so validating when you have the honor and privilege of working with people for many years, and you can see the development of individuals and what they choose to do in their life, how they manifest their morphology, and how true and accurate it is over all the years. It's amazing.

Lymphatic's Three Front-Faces
Jupiter/Zeus

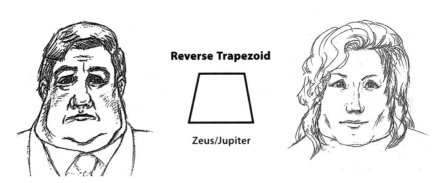

Reverse Trapezoid

Zeus/Jupiter

Fig. 2.18. Male and female Jupiter/Zeus with
corresponding reverse trapezoid shape

The Jupiter front-face shape is considered a reverse trapezoid that is wider at the bottom but with a broad forehead (see figure 2.18, above).

Winston Churchill is a prime example. Jupiter types are the most objective thinkers and visionaries, and they have an uncanny ability to see the larger picture of how things are and how they can become. They tend to be ritualistic, benevolent, and quite devotional with strong religious feelings, and while they are typically tolerant, receptive, and passive, they can also be dogmatic and authoritarian. They require justice and tend to be good moderators. Characteristically, they have a double chin and need to be a little bit overweight for their health.

Moon/Ios

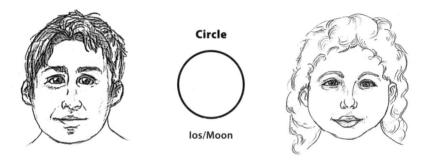

Fig. 2.19. Male and female Moon/Ios with
corresponding circle shape

Another Lymphatic front-face shape is the circle or Moon (see figure 2.19, above), round and full, just like the full moon, which can be seen in Truman Capote. They have medium blue eyes.

The Moon type is considered moody, dreamy, and can follow the moon's rhythm of waxing and waning. It is interesting for the Moon type to note that they have the most strength when the Moon is full and the least strength when it is new. Thus, they should take it slow during the new moon. Moon people should be about ten pounds overweight to be healthy. However, if they weigh much more, it can lead to depression due to water retention. The antidote is vitamin B$_6$.

The Moon mother is considered the most maternal of women and is most associated with being a strong mother. Moon mothers tend to be good childbearers and -rearers. The man in a Moon mother's life often takes second place to her children.

Like Mercury types, Moons tend to be performers, dancers, and singers. One example is Linda Ronstadt.

Neptune/Poseidon

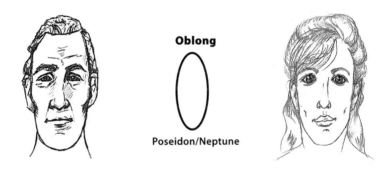

Fig. 2.20. Male and female Neptune/Poseidon with corresponding oblong shape

The Neptune front-face is an oblong, capsule shape (see figure 2.20, above). Good examples are Stan Laurel and Carl Reiner. Neptunes typically have light blue eyes. Sometimes the oblong Neptune shape can be connected with the Nervous type who may have a bullet or cone-shaped back of the head.

Neptunes are the most spiritual of all types. They tend to be guided by their early spiritual experiences and can spend their life trying to recapture that experience. They also tend to be extremely artistic. Generally, they are musically talented. They are often musicians or artists and are very creative. You often see them as piano players or vocalists. Duke Ellington and Cher are examples. They are also excellent dancers, and they tend to enjoy experimentation in the bedroom. While they tend to be gregarious and fun, they often have trouble holding on to and understanding relationships.

Neptune types, being associated with the Lymphatic temperament, tend to be paunchy. They also tend toward baldness. As occurs in the nebulous nature of the Neptune atmosphere, Neptune has trouble seeing things clearly, especially relationships. It is like looking through water. The Neptune body tends to move slowly. Since they have multiple distractions, they can have real difficulty forming stable relationships.

A Collection of Real-Life Front-Faces

It is time to roll up your sleeves and train your eye. In this section, we will review the front-faces with examples of people in the public eye. Because these people are so well known, finding images of them should be relatively easy. If you look at pictures of some of the people mentioned here, you may notice that the angle of the photo, whether or not the person is smiling, and the relative age of the person when the picture was taken all influence the appearance of the front-face. Especially note that with age and gravity or as jowls form, the face may change shape. We also see this dramatically when one gains or loses weight. Please keep these points in mind when viewing the photographs. It bears repeating at this point that morphology is both a science and an art, so you are encouraged to respect your intuition and honor the impressions you receive upon first glance.

Typical Planetary Types

The following is a list of a variety of famous typical planetary types. Note that because of the homogenization of American culture, you might not see the pure, typical planetary geometrical shapes mentioned above in these faces, but you will see combinations. (Likewise, while in pure morphological types the temperament and one of its associated front-faces will be together on the same person, you can expect to see a variety of mixes in which a front-face of one temperament will appear with the profile of another temperament type.*) As you observe more and more faces, you will start to recognize the nuances of these combinations. For instance, someone might have a Sun forehead and a Saturn bottom face. These combinations are indicated in the list below when two planets are mentioned as one over the other, meaning one planet is seen on the top part of the face and the other on the bottom.

> The classic face for an actress is Venus. It is considered the most beautiful female face. As regards male actors, the Saturn is very popular. In both cases the casting director will consciously or unconsciously cast the shape of the face to match the role.

Woody Allen, actor, is a short Mercury.

Fred Astaire, actor/dancer, is a long Mercury.

Drew Barrymore, actress, is a Saturn with Venus overtones.

Richard Belzer, comedian/actor, is a Saturn.

Charles Bronson, actor, is an Earth.

Yul Brynner, actor, is a Sun.

Nicholas Cage, actor, is a Venus over long Mercury.

James Cagney, actor, is an Earth.

Truman Capote, novelist, is a Moon.

Drew Carey, actor, is a Jupiter over Pluto.

Winston Churchill, politician, is a Jupiter.

George Clooney, actor, is a Saturn.

James Dean, actor, is a Saturn.

Bob Dylan, singer, is a Venus.

John Glenn, astronaut, is a Sun.

Sean Hayes, actor, is a Saturn.

Stan Laurel, actor, is a Neptune.

Jude Law, actor, is a Saturn.

Jennifer Lopez, entertainer, is a Sun with mild Venus overtones.

---

*For more on this see "Temperament Type: Pure or Mixed?" starting on page 166.

Lyle Lovett, singer, is a Saturn on the edge of Uranus.

Madonna, entertainer, is a Venus with Mercury overtones.

Megan Mullally, actress, is a Mars over Venus.

Edward R. Murrow, broadcast journalist, is a Uranus.

Oprah, TV personality, is a Moon over Venus.

Brad Pitt, actor, is a Pluto.

Ronald Reagan, actor/president, is a Mars.

Robert Redford, actor, is a Venus.

Burt Reynolds, actor, is a Mars over Venus.

Christina Ricci, actress, is a Venus.

Julia Roberts, actress, is a Saturn.

Ginger Rogers, actress, is a Pluto.

Tony Shalhoub, actor, is a Mars.

Meryl Streep, actress, is a Uranus.

Elizabeth Taylor, actress, is a Venus.

Chuck Yeager, astronaut, is a Sun.

All about the Forehead

As mentioned earlier, the front-face modifies the temperament. Let us now examine the modifiers of the front-face, the forehead in particular. Remember that the face is holographic as is the entire body. That is, the face contains and reflects the whole person. We can see the physical, emotional, mental, social, and moral aspects of each individual all in the face. When looking at the face, notice the forehead and familiarize yourself with its eight possible planetary shapes, which are shown in figure 2.21 (on the following page) and described in more detail in the list that follows.

- When a forehead is oval, it is a Sun forehead. It has a domed appearance as contrasted with the curve of the Moon forehead, which is wider, and the Neptune, which is narrower.
- When the person has a lozenge or heart-shaped face, and the dome is curved as an arc, it is considered a Venus forehead.

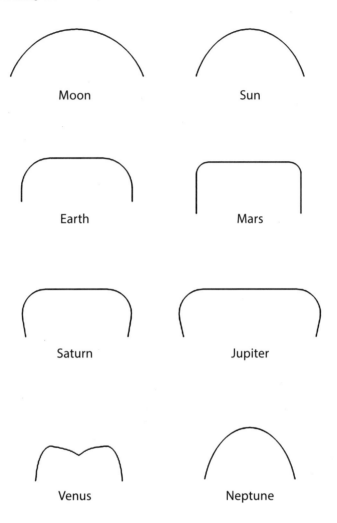

Moon

Sun

Earth

Mars

Saturn

Jupiter

Venus

Neptune

Fig. 2.21. Forehead and hairline shapes

- When the forehead is rectangular, and the hairline is straight across the top, the forehead is associated with Mars.
- When the forehead is square and squat, it is associated with the Earth type.
- When the forehead is broad and fanned-out, it is a Jupiter forehead, which generally is demonstrative of the visionary type. When this shape is narrower, it is a Saturn forehead.

The forehead is defined as the area that goes from the eyebrow to the hairline. If people have lost their hairline, you must estimate where the hairline would have been.

You will often notice that women tend to keep their foreheads covered. This is interesting since the forehead tends to be the expression of a person's power. When a woman has to interact in a way that shows she is not hiding or weak, she should show her forehead to indicate her power.

Episodic Depression Appearing in the Forehead and Mouth of a Young Woman

Once, when a new patient came into my office and I looked at her face, I thought, "Uh oh. I don't know what brought this young college student here, but I am concerned about her in terms of depression or possibly bipolar disorder."

That was the intuitive hit I received from her when I shook her hand. I invited her into the room, and she said her chief complaint was episodic depression. Her hope was to see me as a nutritionist and find out about food allergies and so forth because the mind, she said, can be so affected by what we eat.

Just looking at a person, you can receive a sense about what's going on for them. In this case, the woman's triangularis muscles (described later in chapter 4) in her lip were pointed down. For a young woman, it is unusual for the lower lip to turn down. She also had a flatness to her forehead. In my experience, when I see a full, large forehead, and it is smooth and pouching out, but not in a Bilious way, and the hairline is very rounded and full, I see a person with a degree of manic depression.

I did not mention this to her because, for obvious reasons, I did not want to plant this idea in her. As my teacher, Dr. Gerald Epstein, often said, "We are 100 percent suggestible, 100 percent of the time," so you don't give any diagnoses, any labels, or any titles. In reading her morphology, I felt that my understanding was confirmed when she said her visit was about her complaint of depression and anxiety.

In general, and specifically in the forehead, roundness represents female qualities, receptivity, passivity, emotionality, and dreaminess, while angular lines signify male qualities, aggressiveness, and intellect. Round faces in general are more emotive, while angular faces are quieter, less emotive, and not really concerned with the dream life.

Here are three points about the forehead: First, it can help you read the temperament, which is evaluated when viewing the profile. Second, it is the top third of the face, which represents one's intellectual strength. Third, the hairline helps determine the front-face shape.

I want to note again that it is common for women to wear their hair covering all or part of their forehead. This habit possibly has been established culturally because women have been conditioned not to show their power. I say again, it is better to show it. When we see hair growing into the forehead, this growth can restrict that person's intellectual functions. Also, I might mention that a widow's peak tends to make a person attractive to the opposite sex, as it reflects a point of charm.

The hairline can be described as straight or irregular, and follows an angular, dome, rectilinear, or heart shape depending on the front-face type. For example, the forehead of Mars and Saturn are considered angular types, with the more rectangle-shaped forehead of Mars being associated with more aggressiveness. The Jupiter forehead is described as broad, wide, and deep, as seen in Albert Einstein and Abraham Lincoln (see figures 2.22 and 2.23). Einstein's forehead is considered square, but the broadness speaks to Jupiter, which is considered the visionary type. I had a patient, a woman, with a beautiful Jupiter forehead, and when I asked her if she was a visionary, she said, "Yes, I work at Disney."

The dome, or arch-shaped hairline, is associated with the Sun type and is considered idealistic. In contrast, a square hairline speaks to material practicality; this type is not philosophical. The heart-shaped forehead is associated with Venus.

The round forehead is considered feminine while a linear forehead

Fig. 2.22. Abraham Lincoln
(Photo taken in the Lincoln–Douglas debates, May 7, 1858)

Fig. 2.23. Albert Einstein
(Photo by Orren Jack Turner, 1947)

is considered masculine. Round foreheads—Moons and Neptunes, for example—are receptive and idealistic, and linear foreheads are considered aggressive. Each of these shapes imbues the forehead with the quality that is associated with the face type, and we can glean much from the simplest glance at the forehead.

When we look at the forehead, we can look at it in relationship to the whole face shape, the big face, the little face, or the three zones. We must also address the forehead's musculature and its shape, slants, and zones.

Each of the three zones of the face can be further divided into three sections in the same way: intellectual, emotional, and material. When there are prominences on the forehead, we look to see which zone they are in. When evaluating this aspect of the forehead, it is helpful to turn your attention briefly from the front-face to the profile (see figure 2.24). Each prominence limits or enhances the qualities of that zone. For example, if the prominence is found in the brow, which is the material zone, it speaks to increases in material wants and to a possible loss of intellectual function. If the prominence is in the mid-zone it can speak to a person's increased emotionality. If the prominence is in the top zone it can speak to the person's intellect. The nature of the prominence can also affect the zones. For example, it could be bumpy or smooth—a bump indicating that there is something happening in that zone.

Here are some examples of forehead characteristics and the qualities they suggest. Note that for determining the slope, or slant, of a forehead, you again want to look at the profile along with the front-face.

- If you are looking to hire or need an analytical thinker, an ideal forehead is a Mars, which is angular, a quality of the Sanguine temperament. The Saturn forehead, while it is not Sanguine, can still be analytical due to its angular nature.
- If the forehead slopes back sharply, it speaks to quick reactions and being a risk taker. People with this slope can fly off the handle and have a firecracker first response.

Prominence in the
material zone

Prominence in the
emotional zone

Prominence in the
intellectual zone

Fig. 2.24. Forehead prominence: material, emotional,
and intellectual zones

- A moderate, oblique slant backward, where the angle of the forehead is about 30° to 40°, is seen in individuals who must take action. And while they are action-oriented, they can think appropriately about what needs to be done and offer a considered response.
- Individuals with a straight forehead exhibit a balance between thoughtfulness and action.
- When the slope of the forehead is a negative angle, meaning it pouches forward, the person may have a potential to be a genius.
- Individuals with irregular foreheads can have something "off" in their intellectual ability and awry in their thinking. An example

of irregularity is when one side of the forehead is more prominent than the other.

- If the temples pouch out, you do not see great reservoirs of energy in these individuals.
- Individuals with a smooth, wrinkle-free forehead can process information in but not out.
- When you see individuals with furrows in the forehead, these are people who think very deeply. If there are vertical furrows or lines, this indicates concentrating on one point or thought.
- When you see a vein running vertically down the middle of the forehead, that individual wants to find an adventure. In fact, when I ask my patients who have that vertical vein, "Do you like adventure?" every one of them says, "Yes!"
- A prominent ridge over the eyebrow speaks to materialism.
- When the forehead is pouched out, the person does not feel very deeply, and is a reactor.
- If a person has a sunken area in the forehead, the person's wave goes in—the person is a feeling type.
- A person with a bony forehead can be introverted, and if there is a hollowness in the forehead he or she can become agitated but cannot act.
- A vertical forehead indicates a prudent person with stability between mind and action.
- If the forehead is straight and narrow, one can be considered narrow-minded.
- If the forehead is rectangular with wrinkles, the person can be objective and have strength of mind.
- A person with a round forehead might be considered childlike.

Seeing Colors Clearly

When we first introduced looking at the face, we mentioned that certain colors can help us diagnostically to understand what is happening in the body. However, we do not want to misinterpret the meaning of the color. For instance, while we might associate jaundice with yellow, a *slight* yellow hue on a Mercury is considered normal. Thus, it's important to keep in mind each temperament's native color: brown for Bilious, yellow for Nervous, red for Sanguine, and white for Lymphatic.

Equally important, we need to know that there are colors associated with the organs as follows: liver is orange, lungs are pink, thyroid is blue, gallbladder is green, kidneys are yellow, heart and vascular system are red, intestines are brown, the lymphatic network is white, and eyes and brain are gray. These correspondences are based on ancient revelations.

The purpose of introducing these colors is to help an individual utilize such bits of information when perhaps doing an imagery exercise. Imagery in the hands of a skilled face morphologist can help with a patient's inner life. Further, as we know, due to the law of reciprocity, a correction in the inner life would then be reflected in the outer life, and consequently you would see a change in the person's face.

The following imagery exercise provides an inner process for scanning your body for possible health changes as opposed to looking in the mirror, which is an outer process of scanning.*

Body Scan Visualization

Sit upright. Breathe out and in three times with each exhalation longer than the inhalation. Close your eyes. See, sense, and feel yourself miniaturizing and traveling through your entire body from top to bottom and bottom to top. Make note of any colors, shapes, or distortions you may see. When you're done, come out of the body and return to full size. Open your eyes.

---

*To learn more about mental imagery, please refer to *Healing Visualizations: Creating Health through Imagery* by Dr. Gerald Epstein.

In addition to the fact that each of the organs and front-faces has a resonant color, Dr. Epstein taught that each day of the week is also associated with a color. They are as follows:

- Monday is any pastel color.
- Tuesday is red.
- Wednesday is silver-gray blue.
- Thursday is blue or purple.
- Friday is bright green.
- Saturday is brown or black.
- Sunday is yellow.

This information can also be used to assist in healing. If one finds that a person has a weakness or deficiency in a color or an organ, one could ask the person to wear a scarf of that color on the day of the week that corresponds with that color. For example, if the person's body scan visualization reveals that they need the color yellow, ask them to wear a yellow scarf or yellow clothing on Sunday. Wearing the day's corresponding color imbues body and mind with the attributes of that color.

The colors have the following meanings, based on their planetary correspondences (see the following section and the facing table "Planets and Their Associated Colors and Numbers").

While not a planetary color, white represents light, goodness, innocence, purity, and virginity.

COLORS AND THEIR MEANINGS

Color	Meaning
Purple/Violet	Spiritually attuned, strong emotional life, royalty
Silver	Reflection of gold, healing
Black	The unknown, inner self, the sacred, evil, mystery, death
Green	Victory, life, relaxing, tranquil, growth

Color	Meaning
Red	Strength, power, life blood, comfort, heat
Orange	Female strength
Blue	Healing, wards off evil, joy, vitality, divine light, true blue
Yellow	Intellect, generosity, open, optimistic, cheerfulness, sociability
Brown	Intestinal
Gray	Guilt, caution, herd mentality, conservative, neutral, foggy

Planets, Colors, Numbers, and Their Meanings

In the Western spiritual tradition there is a system of numerology where numbers have specific meanings. In the case of face morphology, the front-faces are associated with planets and have a number assigned to them as well as an associated color. Once you evaluate the front-face and establish the planetary shape, you can then proceed to the table below, which shows the color and number assigned to each shape. Once that is done, then proceed to the next table, which gives the meaning of the number. Now you can tell the individual, or see within yourself, the way your life is going as is understood by numerology.

PLANETS AND THEIR ASSOCIATED COLORS AND NUMBERS

Planet	Color	Number
Neptune	Purple/Violet	1
Uranus	Silver	2
Saturn	Black	3
Jupiter	Green	4
Mars	Red	5
Sun	Orange	6

PLANETS AND THEIR
ASSOCIATED COLORS AND NUMBERS *(continued)*

Planet	Color	Number
Venus	Blue	7
Mercury	Yellow	8
Moon	Silver	9
Pluto	Silver	9
Earth	Brown and gray	10

The table that follows lists numbers from 1 to 20 plus 22 and 33*
and their meanings, which you can apply to the shape of the front-face.
You may find that these number associations can represent challenges
that a person may work on throughout her or his life. For example, if a
person has a Pluto front-face, they are a 9 and might have difficulty with
completion. Note that in numerology numbers above 10 are reduced to
a single digit. For example, 14 is reduced to 5 (1 + 4 = 5). So a person
with a Mars front-face can look at both 5 and 14 for insight.

NUMBERS AND THEIR MEANINGS

Number	Meaning
1	Unity, generator of All from All
2	Divisiveness
3	Synthesis
4	Construction, home and family, career
5	Creativity, generosity, and materialistic interest
6	Construction on a higher level, joy
7	Ambivalence and growth cycle, possibility for freedom
8	Nagging unresolved patterns from the past, infinity, new beginning

*In traditional numerology 22 and 33 are considered master numbers.

Number	Meaning
9	Completion
10	Perfection in everyday life
11	Divided self
12	Wisdom
13	Good fortune
14	Fellowship
15	Fulfillment of purposes in life
16	Death
17	Happiness
18	Life
19	Benedictions, blessings from above
20	Difficulty in marriage
22	Auspiciousness
33	Spiritual relationships

Traditional Chinese Medicine: Another Tradition That Reads the Front-Face

Now that you are tuning into the messages hidden within front-faces, let us look at another system that also reads the face. In addition to being a face morphologist and a chiropractor, I am also an acupuncturist. I would like to introduce you to Traditional Chinese Medicine (TCM) in the context of face reading. Although it is not part of face morphology, it is a useful complement.

While TCM is an entirely different system, to those practitioners who utilize it, you may be able to incorporate in your face reading an understanding of what is happening in the rest of the body by paying attention to the relationship between the meridians that run through the face and the morphological significance of those locations. And to those who have never been exposed to the five elements, here is a taste of it to whet your appetite.

We've already seen that there is much to be observed in the color, shape, skin tone, projections, indentations, concavities, and convexities of the face. All have meaning. Each of these components gives you a sense of a person's morphological type.

Now, I want to return to color again. Imagine that you are looking at a face where the nose and cheeks are beet red. This tells you that this person is a Sanguine with a passionate nature. Being that the nose and cheeks are in the emotional zone you can surmise that the Sanguine may be dealing with emotionality around intense relationships. (*Caution:* You also must look at heart health whenever you see a beet red nose.)

In Traditional Five Element Chinese Medicine and TCM, colors are associated with each of the elements and can reflect an individual's *chi,* which is the energy of their health. The five elements and their colors are as follows: wood, which is green; earth, which is yellow; metal, which is gray; water, which is black; and fire, which is red. In Chinese face reading, when you observe the color that appears around the eyes, for example, you can determine whether a person has an elemental weakness. For this reason, if a person comes into my office with graying underneath their eyes, I would look to their breathing, because I know that in Traditional Chinese Medicine gray is the color of metal, metal goes to the lungs, and thus, the lungs might have breathing or allergy issues.

The Chinese truths about face color have been known for thousands of years, and people have been able to read these glyphs over and over again. It is interesting to note that there is a common understanding that when a child presents with black or gray rings under or around the eyes, it can be called an "allergy shiner." In the context of TCM, such details make sense.

Those who are interested can study Five Element theory on their own. For the tempted, however, here are two cursory overviews of the relationships among the five elements:

First, there are the creative and controlling cycles known as Shen and Ko respectively (see figure 2.25).

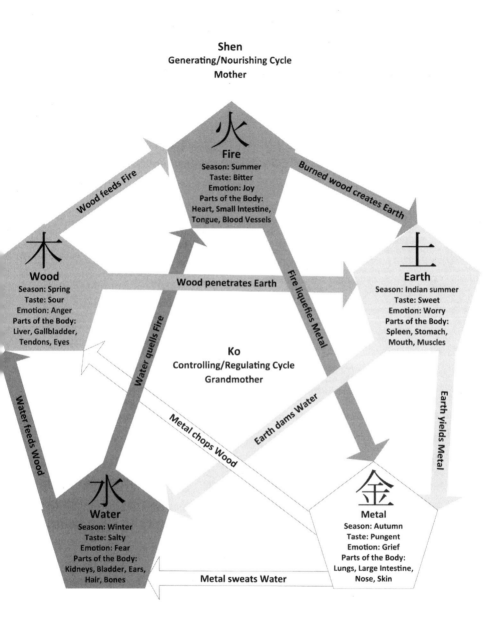

Fig. 2.25. TCM Five Elements:
Generating and Controlling Cycles

- Creative/Shen: Wood feeds fire; fire creates earth; earth creates metal; metal sweats water; water feeds wood.
- Controlling/Ko: Water quells fire; fire liquefies metal; metal chops wood; wood penetrates earth; earth dams water.

Second, the organs are associated with the five elements and their colors as follows:

- The heart is associated with fire (red).
- The spleen and pancreas are associated with earth (yellow).
- The lungs are associated with metal (gray).
- The kidneys are associated with water (black).
- The liver is associated with wood (green).

Another way that TCM makes diagnoses is by understanding that qualities of temperature are associated with health. For instance, since we know from TCM that the tip of the nose is related to the heart, if you look at the tip of the nose and see that it is very red, you can conclude that the heart has heat. This is an indicator of ill health and the person may need a referral. There are a number of correlations between TCM and face morphology, and the view that the tip of the nose is associated with the heart is one of them.

There are many different facial clues in TCM that can guide you to understanding the organ systems and the general health of an individual. I am sure, for example, that many people recognize the clue (as is understood in both Eastern and Western medicine) that yellow eyes can indicate jaundice.

Remember, every part of the body can be read as a hologram representing the whole body within it. The face is a representation of our entire being. As I mentioned before, it can be helpful to look at some of the ways that other cultures, nations, and traditions approach morphology, and you can now see that TCM is also a contributor.

A Quick Recap
for Assessing the Face

As we have seen, the face has many aspects to be read and it might be helpful here to briefly recap a few of them.

The temperament is read from the profile, and from this you get the general archetypes of Bilious, Nervous, Sanguine, and Lymphatic. While everyone has all four temperaments, there are degrees of each. As we have frequently noted, we list them as primary, secondary, tertiary, and quaternary. Combining the back of the head shape with the profile can confirm one's primary temperament.

- When the back of the head is shaped like a bowling ball, this indicates a Bilious temperament.
- When the back of the head is shaped like a cone or a bullet, this indicates a Nervous temperament.
- When the back of the head is shaped like a spatula, this indicates a Sanguine temperament.
- When the back of the neck is prominent and thick enough to be considered a trapezoid, this indicates a Lymphatic temperament.

Understanding that the temperaments are associated intimately with their embryological derivations, and then knowing the conditions that support that embryological layer, we can extrapolate characteristics for each temperament. For example, the mesoderm layer cannot resist a bacterial infection easily, and in the mesoderm an infection spreads very fast. Since a mesoderm type is Sanguine, the Sanguine must be careful to act swiftly when they do get an infection.

The front-face reveals its counterpart for the personality based on its planetary shape: Saturn, Earth, Uranus, Mercury, Long Mercury, Mars, Pluto, Venus, Sun, Jupiter, Moon, and Neptune.

Another way to discern something about the face is through the measurement (or size) of the big face—all the flesh of the face including the circumference of the head—in relation to the little face—the eyes, nose, and lips, which we call the receptors.

Just as the intention of health is balance and harmony, one can see the face and determine if there is disharmony. *Heal, whole, health,* and *holy* all have the same root. As we will see in the next chapter, certain exercises can create harmony. For example, if one has a down-turning of the lips, it can represent bitterness. An appropriate physical exercise would be for the person to lift both sides of the lips with the fingers. Then, due to the law of reciprocity, when the lifting of the lips corrects the lip downturn, the person becomes less bitter.

Each temperament is also associated with a color: Bilious is considered swarthy or olive-toned, Nervous is yellow, Sanguine is red, and Lymphatic is white. However, even though one might have rosy cheeks and seem to be of Sanguine temperament, this color could be imposed upon a yellow Nervous temperament or a swarthy Bilious temperament from a brisk walk in cold air. So to confirm the complexion in relation to temperament, one would look at the palm of the person's hand since it is not as exposed to climate (see "Palm Color" in chapter 5).

As for eye color, another important characteristic, this is generally associated with a face's particular planetary shape. For example, Mars is usually an icy, light blue, while Pluto is a deep, violet blue. Sun has green with occasional yellow flecks, and Venus might have deep, blue eyes but can also have brown eyes. And, of course, most of the other shapes can have brown eyes too. Bilious and Lymphatic types are brown in general but can be any color, and the Nervous types— Mercury and Long Mercury—typically have brown eyes. Blue-eyed people are most often associated with the Sanguine type. The piercing blue eyes of Pluto mean the person is very deep. The cold, blue eyes of Mars mean they can freeze you out or be distant.

Remember to also consider the three zones of the face: the upper third from the hairline to the eyebrows, which is considered the intellectual zone; the middle third from the bridge of the nose to the bottom of the nose, which is considered the emotional zone; and the lower third from the lower lip to the tip of the chin, which is considered the physical or concrete zone. Everyone is an individual and might have any particular color, tone, characteristic, shape, or size of their zones. Understanding these nuances can bring deeper insight into the personality and health of each individual.

3

Reading the
Facial Features

The front-face can be considered a changeable persona. In a way, the front-face is a mask: it changes as you inscribe character traits upon it.

The profile, which reveals the temperament, communicates a great deal about the individual. But when you look at the front-face and you have an "Aha!" moment, you will realize that that is the way a face is to be read—in an instantaneous glance. The aim is not to study. The aim is to look quickly and see what grabs your attention. It may be the nose, the eyes, or the ears. Whichever it is, you will intuitively make an instant assessment. For instance, when you see a roundness of the features, you can say it is expressed in a Moon way. When you see a broadness to the forehead and the features, you can say it is expressed in a Jupiter way. In general, once you know the characteristics that we have described regarding front-faces, you can read the features of any face quickly and accurately.

In this chapter, we are looking specifically at the individual features, which modify the front-face and tell us so much more about each individual.

The Meaning and Shape of the Eyes

We all know the saying that the eyes are the window to the soul. You might also say that they tell us about emotionality. Not only is the face

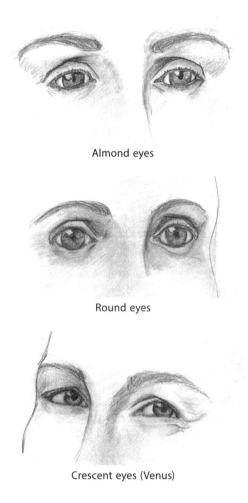

Almond eyes

Round eyes

Crescent eyes (Venus)

Fig. 3.1. Eye shapes: almond, round, and crescent

holographic, but every feature is a hologram of the whole being. In fact, some people can become expert at reading one particular feature and can read the whole glyph of the human being in that feature. To begin, we focus on the meaning found in the shape of the eyes.

The eyes often reflect what is going on emotionally and internally with an individual. The shape of the eye is either almond, round, or semi-round (see figure 3.1, above). An almond-shaped eye often speaks to intelligence and emotional strength. The round eye might be considered a sign of emotional difficulty. It may also speak to dreaminess and to a lack of focus. A round Moon eye can signify a tendency toward depression. Even so, round eyes can take in a lot, particularly since they have been associated with emotional lability.

The semi-round eye, also known as the crescent or half-moon eye, is associated with the Venus type. Remember that whenever any of the individual features take on the shape of a particular planetary name—for instance, Moon or Venus or Sun—then the qualities that we have spoken about when examining those planetary faces are also part of those features.

Eyes also have a tilt. When the medial portion of the eye is turned up, it speaks to optimism. When the medial portion of the eye is turned down, it speaks to pessimism. The eye that is straight across is regarded as even-tempered. If the outer part of the eye has an exaggerated upward tilt, that individual might struggle with adulterous thoughts. This does not mean only in a sexual way. Adultery in this context can mean not being able to focus on one thing. For example, you might see that people have never cheated on their partners, but that they frequently engage in three-way relationships with friends or family where there is always a side to be taken. If the eye has a downward tilt on the outside, the individual is considered dreamy or seductive and also a little self-involved; this can also indicate depression.

Bedroom Eyes

Sometimes you see "bedroom eyes," or the eyes that slant upward. I saw this once with a female patient who came in with a blood dyscrasia (an imbalance in the blood). It was an interesting situation. I don't know why, but when I've seen people with blood dyscrasias, they seem to be in adulterous situations in their lives. I can't confirm that this is the case with every blood dyscrasia sufferer, but it's an observation that I've made. So I brought it up and asked, "Do you find yourself triangulating?" (I don't say "committing adultery.") And she asked, "What does that

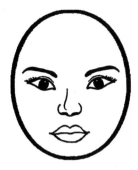

mean?" I said, "You have two friends, and you are the third, and you have to pick one or the other because of a dispute, and you find yourself stuck and not knowing which way to go." And she said, "As a matter of fact, I'm dating a married man, and I'm married." The nature is in the face. It opens up all these revelations.

Evaluate the protrusion of the eye by viewing it from the side. If you see the sclera and iris pointing out, and the eye is beyond the lid, this is exophthalmos, which is seen in hyperthyroidism. One may see a protrusion from the front, but this is a pseudo-protrusion. It must be evaluated from the side.

When someone has huge receptors, they may report that they are overwhelmed by sensory input. It is recommended that they squint their eyes to diminish the sensory input from the outside.

Something else to note is the interpupillary distance—that is, the distance between the pupils. When the interpupillary distance is small (the eyes are close together), that often speaks to emotional instability or being focused or narrow-minded. If the interpupillary distance is large (the eyes are far apart), that can also speak to emotional instability but in a different way. The person can be too trusting and without boundaries. It can also indicate generosity, open-mindedness, or even gullibility. An example of a large interpupillary distance is seen in children with fetal alcohol syndrome.

Wide-eyed people are typically slow to react, and when the upper lid hangs low over the iris, it indicates unreliability.

The Color of the Eyes

As we have noted before, eye color is generally associated with a particular planet. Eyes that are considered blue are often associated with the Sanguine type (Mars, Venus, Sun, Pluto). Eyes that are considered to be in the brown family are usually associated with Bilious (Saturn, Uranus, Earth). Any front-face can have any color eyes, but certain planetary types demonstrate notable consistencies: Green eyes with yellow flecks are generally associated with Sun types, but note that Sun-shaped front-faces that come from Scandinavia are typically blue-eyed. When we see very dark clear blue eyes, we associate them with Venus. Brown eyes are also often seen in the Venus type as well as in the Mercury type. Pale blue eyes or even hazel eyes, which are often associated with dreaminess, are considered Moon.

The Moon or the Mars shape can also have ice-blue eyes. And when you see those ice-blue eyes, they generally have a feeling of detachment or coldness. Very dark, deep blue eyes, that almost have the feeling of piercing through, are considered Pluto eyes.

Sanpaku eyes, meaning "three whites," where the white is visible on the sides and the bottom, can indicate a loss of energy and quite possibly a movement toward death.

Reading the Eyebrows

Each eyebrow is divided into three parts—medial, middle, and lateral. The medial part relates to the bridge that connects the right and left frontal bone and the nose; the middle is in the center, just over the pupil of the eye; and the lateral is the farthest away from the center. When observing the eyebrows, you look at the length of each of the three zones, and from these three pieces you can tell the entire character of the person.

You also look for the amount of hair in the eyebrow, whether it is bushy, thin, regular, or irregular. If the hair has a certain thickness and bushiness, it reveals good stamina. Whenever we see the lateral third of the eyebrow missing it always correlates with thyroid issues. The thinning and loss of hair on this part of the eyebrow may indicate developing hypo-thyroidism. Also, when one has thick eyebrows and they become thin, consider the possibility that the genital system might have been affected.

It is interesting to note that just as plastic surgery or hair coloring can affect the expression of a type, hair implants can also be used to make corrections to the eyebrows.

Figure 3.2, on the next page, shows the ten basic eyebrow shapes. A rounded or curved eyebrow represents more than ordinary persever-ance and endurance and has a female quality. A straight line or angular thrust shows a dissipation of energy. When the medial portion of the eyebrow is angled toward the nose, it is seen as indicating a normal rela-tionship with others. If it is straight and horizontal toward the bridge, you may see that relationships with others are in doubt. If it is angled up and away toward the forehead, the person might manifest suspicion. If the eyebrow is curved and there is a big distance between it and the eyelid, it indicates that that person can be clever.

If the middle portion of the eyebrow is straight horizontal, it is con-sidered balanced. If it is convex with the bow up toward the forehead, it signifies a dissipation of energy. If angled up toward the forehead, it signifies people who take on new projects and plans and who may seek retribution from others. If the middle portion of the eyebrow is angled to look like an upside-down *V,* this is considered a mercurial eyebrow and indicates quick thought and wit. Also, if there is a stack of hair above the middle portion of the eyebrow, it is said that that person has a lot on their mind.

When the lateral aspect of the eyebrow is angled downward, it is considered balanced. If it is straight across, like a horizontal line, it rep-resents stubbornness. If angled upward, it may indicate irresponsibility. If convex, with an angle down, where the eyebrow goes down to the level of the outer conjunctiva, the person is considered self-absorbed.

As you can see, the outer third of the eyebrow has four directions.

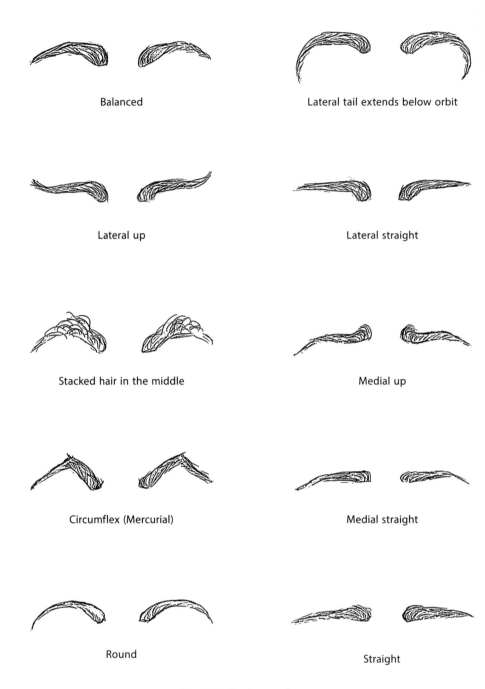

Balanced

Lateral tail extends below orbit

Lateral up

Lateral straight

Stacked hair in the middle

Medial up

Circumflex (Mercurial)

Medial straight

Round

Straight

Fig. 3.2. Eyebrow shapes

When you see the hair of the eyebrow extend down past the lateral corner of the eye, and even past the orbit of the eye, it's considered an extreme downward position and indicates a person who can be so self-absorbed that they can have trouble maintaining relationships.

Bony eyebrows, where the bone protrudes, are thought to signify an extroverted person, while flat eyebrow bones are thought to signify an introverted person.

Eyebrows Grew below the Orbit

I had a patient who had eyebrows that grew down below the orbit, which indicates self-absorption, and indeed, the man was completely obsessed with himself. I recommended that he tweeze his brows up, because he was a police officer, and he wanted to have more compassion and not be so concerned about himself. Removing this part of the eyebrow helped. He shaved it, but tweezing was the recommendation.

Bilious Saturn eyebrows are characteristically thick. If they go fully across the head they are known as "synophrys" in the medical field and commonly called "unibrow"—they can create a barrier between the intellectual and emotional zones. When you see this in patients who are having difficulty in relationships, you may advise them—especially men—to tweeze the middle of the brows to open up emotionally by connecting the emotional zone with the intellectual zone.

Unibrow

A patient, when he first came to me, was around thirteen-and-a-half years old and was not able to be in the regular school system due to violent tendencies. Because he had a unibrow, there was no open space between his intellectual and emotional zones, so the intellect could not help to curb the emotions and impulses that were out of balance. So I suggested to the mother to tweeze a gap between his eyebrows. She did so and noticed an appreciable difference.

The Cheeks:
Reservoir of Energy

We go from eyes and eyebrows to a short look at cheeks.

The word *cheeks* comes from the Latin meaning "increased reservoir of energy." When you see cheeks that are full and nicely shaped, you can assume the person has strength. Full cheeks can represent a search for honor and glory and are often connected with security and personal importance.

Little Balls in the Cheeks

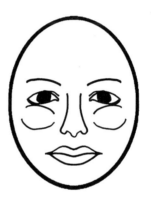

I had a patient who had been coming to me for a very long time. She had little balls in the upper part of her cheeks that puzzled me. I asked Dr. Epstein what it meant, and he said they were cheeks of timidity. I didn't know that, because when I was with her, she was extremely open with me and very clear about what she wanted done. With time, she revealed that she was very timid with other people in her personal life and at work.

There are three types of cheeks: the full cheek, the flat cheek, and the hollow cheek. Of course, there may be variations.

A person with full cheeks is scared of consequences and only has courage to a point. A big and full cheek often speaks to a degree of sexuality and willpower. A cheek that is full and tight, as can be seen in Sophia Lauren and the young Faye Dunaway, can represent strong will.

A person with a flat cheek is not scared when confronted with something scary. A person with such a cheek, as seen in the older Faye Dunaway, depends on his or her own ingenuity and speed of action and reaction. Due to the lack of power of the flat cheek, such a person tends to use their quick wit. If someone hurts a child with this cheek, it will create a desire for revenge.

A person with a hollow cheek, as seen in Clint Eastwood, is fearless and not troubled by much. Another example is Humphrey Bogart. People with hollow cheeks cannot be led, and one must speak to them gently. Saturn types with indented cheeks—in other words, an indented hollow cheek—like to correct the ills of the world. Sometimes they will take on the whole world.

Dimples in smiling cheeks represent a whimsical and childlike nature.

The Nose:
Spine of the Face

The bone of the nose is considered the spinal column of the face, and the entire face is organized around the nose as the body is organized around the spine. When looking at the nose from the front (see figure 3.3 on the next page), since it is in the middle of the emotional zone, the center of the face, it is prominent and easily observed upon a quick glance. So what might stand out to us are things like the concavity or convexity and the broadness or narrowness of the nasal bone; the shape of the tip of the nose; bumps, lesions, freckles, moles, or whatever features or irregularities might catch our attention. These specifics can reveal much about the person's physical and emotional state. For instance, if one's nose is broad, one is considered steady and strong. If the nose is a narrow pillar, that person is considered emotionally labile. We come in with these aspects as they are inherited through our genetics.

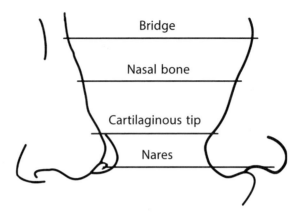

Fig. 3.3. Parts of the nose

The nose and the bridge of the nose speak to emotionality and tolerance. In the following list of characteristics, you'll notice that we revisit the space between the eyes because it also has significance when reading the bridge of the nose.

- A large space between the eyes, when the bridge of the nose is open, represents tolerance and open-mindedness.
- A small space between the eyes that is focused to one point indicates a person who does not see things in a broad way. These people are not typically open and can be considered closed- or narrow-minded.
- A low bridge of the nose indicates primitivity and a person who is instinctually driven.
- A high bridge of the nose indicates intelligence.
- A flat large bridge on the nose means the person is not efficient.
- Hollow bridges, where the space between the root of the nose and the glabella is concave, are seen in efficient people.

Since our learning is founded in repetition, this is a good time to recall that when we viewed the profile, we were establishing the person's temperament. We will do that once more in this process. To see the temperament, we look again at the slope of the forehead, the back of the head, and the angle of the jaw, but now we also consider the profile of the nose. Every nose contains two temperaments because the upper and lower parts of the nose represent different aspects.

As you may remember, earlier I explained that the nose has two main parts: the bony upper part attached to the root (the place where the nose attaches itself to the forehead or glabella), called the nasal bone, and the soft cartilaginous bottom part of the nose, or the bulb, which goes from where the bony part meets the softer lower half to the tip. The nasal bone can be either concave or convex, and the bulb can be either round or straight (aquiline).

If the nasal bone is convex when viewing the profile, like the ones in the two portraits by Leonardo da Vinci shown in figure 3.4, it is a Nervous nose. If it is concave, as it is in the portrait of Winston Churchill on the next page (figure 3.5), it is considered a Lymphatic nose. If it is straight, or aquiline, it is Sanguine. People with a convex nose are concerned with what other people think, which tends

Nervous nose self-portrait   Nervous nose drawing

Fig. 3.4. Nervous nose portraits by Leonardo da Vinci

Fig. 3.5. Lymphatic nose—Winston Churchill (1943)

to influence their choice of work, while people with the concave nose tend to be more calm and less reactive to the world and what it thinks of them. Remember that the Nervous or Lymphatic nose is a fixity, because it is based on the shape of the bone.

The bulb part of the nose is either Bilious or Sanguine. If the bulb is round, it is considered Bilious. As we noted earlier, this Bilious tip tends to indicate people who are friendly and available to others. It is a wonderful attribute for sociability. Karl Malden had that bulbous tip (see figure 3.6).

If the bulb is aquiline it is considered Sanguine. The Sanguine nose tends to indicate a person who is more analytical and less available. Julius Caesar had such a nose (see figure 3.7).

The projection of the nose from the philtrum (the vertical groove below the center of the nose) to the tip of the nose speaks to intelligence. When the projected nose is long, the person is considered

Fig. 3.6. Bilious tip, Karl Malden
(From *On the Waterfront,* 1953)

Fig. 3.7. Aquiline nose
(Eighteenth-century bust of Julius Caesar, British Museum)

highly intelligent, especially if the nose is accompanied by long skinny nostrils.

A person with a pointed nose generally has a quest for learning about humanity. Such people are considered searchers and seekers. And when the nose dips low toward the upper lip, it is considered a conqueror's nose (see figure 3.8).

Fig. 3.8. Conqueror nose
("Profile of an Old Man," by Leonardo da Vinci,
fifteenth century, Uffizi Gallery, Florence)

A Sharp, Long, and Downward-Pointing Nose

I went to the pool and paid the $6.00 entry fee and asked the attendant to please let me have a receipt so I could come back in again later. She said, "No." But the way she said it was very nasty, like she got joy out of it. I quickly looked at her face, and I saw the Wicked Witch of the West. She had that long, sharp, downward-pointing nose! These people like to be conquerors. I didn't take it personally and understood it to simply be her way. This is how we can use face morphology to develop compassion rather than to react defensively.

Figure 3.9 provides just a few nose-combination possibilities. When the temperament that is determined by the jaw and forehead does not exactly match up with the temperament that is read in the nose, we look to the nose as a tempering of the temperament. For example, if a Nervous has a Lymphatic bridge (which is often accomplished by surgery) it takes away the Nervous's ability to pierce the world and adds to their passive nature. If a Bilious (jawline and forehead) has a Sanguine, aquiline tip of the nose, it can take away the congeniality of the temperament and make the individual more analytical and motoric.

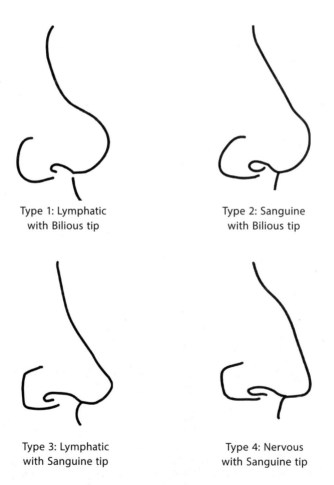

Type 1: Lymphatic
with Bilious tip

Type 2: Sanguine
with Bilious tip

Type 3: Lymphatic
with Sanguine tip

Type 4: Nervous
with Sanguine tip

Fig. 3.9. Nose types

- Type 1: The concave bony part is associated with Lymphatic. The round cartilage is associated with Bilious.
- Type 2: The aquiline bony part is associated with Sanguine. The round cartilage is associated with Bilious.
- Type 3: The concave bony part is associated with Lymphatic. The aquiline tip is associated with Sanguine.
- Type 4: The convex bony part is associated with Nervous. The aquiline tip is associated with Sanguine.

When viewing the nose from the side, if we see a tenting of the nares (see figure 3.10), we have a sign of either envy or jealousy. If there is a tent in the front (the part closer to the tip of the nose) whereby the nostrils go up and form a triangle, this indicates jealousy. If the tent is at the back (the part closer to the maxillary bone), it is envy.

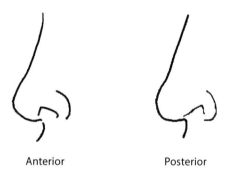

Anterior   Posterior

Fig. 3.10. Tenting of the nares

Nose: Tenting Nares

A patient came into the office, and as I was looking at her profile I saw a tenting of the anterior part of her nares. I said to her, "Do you have any issues with jealousy?" This person immediately started ranting and raving about how jealous she was in her relationship with her husband and how it interfered with her well-being and normal functioning, because she "couldn't bear it." She said that she got too agitated if he got a phone call or any attention from another woman. She just couldn't control herself.

The Philtrum

Now we turn to the small area called the philtrum, the vertical groove in the central space between the nose and upper lip (see figure 3.11). The philtrum can show reserves of strength and amounts of energy. If the groove is deep, there is a good reserve of strength and a lot of energy. If shallow, however, strength and energy dissipate. Lines in the philtrum indicate sexual pride and good humor. A vertical line in the middle of the philtrum represents a sense of humor.

If the distance from the base of the nose to the upper lip is long, these people are motorically active. The projection of the nose from the philtrum to the tip of the nose speaks to intelligence, especially if it is

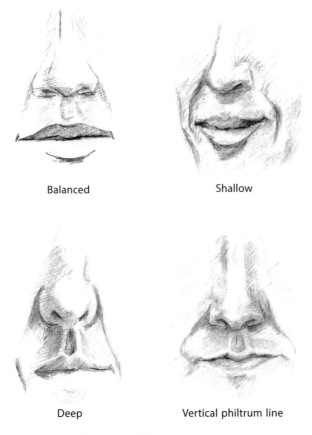

Balanced   Shallow

Deep   Vertical philtrum line

Fig. 3.11. Philtrum types

accompanied by long skinny nostrils. If the nose dips low, obscuring part of the philtrum, the people with this nose are conqueror types.

The Mouth and the Lips

When we speak of the mouth, we include the upper and lower lips and the philtrum. As shown in figure 3.12, mouths can be balanced, forward, flat, or back. Madame Colette Aboulker-Muscat was able to read a person's entire life by just reading the mouth and lips.

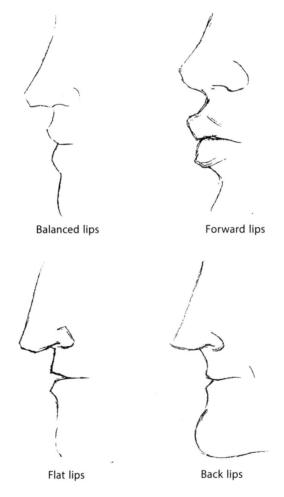

Balanced lips   Forward lips

Flat lips   Back lips

Fig. 3.12. Lip types: side view

Lips: Prankster

Oftentimes, you can see an aspect of personality in the lips. I saw this in a nine-year-old boy, whose lips curled up at the edges. Since that curling can mean mischief, I said to him, "Do you like to play jokes on people?" He totally copped to it and said, "I love doing that!"

Mouth:
Brutality or Gut Issue

I was working with a man who had come in for his lower back, and when I asked him if he wanted me to do the morphology, he said yes. His lower lip was larger than his upper lip. I was concerned because sometimes, when the lip is really jutting out, it can mean brutality. That was a cue to me to be careful with this fellow, but it turned out that when I said to him, "How is your digestion?" he said that he had Crohn's disease. And so, while I wasn't happy that he had Crohn's, I was happy that his protruding lower lip didn't mean brutality, but instead indicated a digestive issue.

When we look at the mouth, we focus on shapes. The upper lip is associated with the individual's relationship to the outside world, the social life, while the lower lip is associated with the relationship to the self and one's biological life. The upper and lower lips together represent the union of the social and physical life. The upper lip relates to sexual glands, the lower lip to bladder, kidneys, and digestion. The tissue of the lip is considered to be associated with the sexual life.

Because the upper lip represents the social life, we look to see if it extends over the lower lip. If it does, then these people are unsure of themselves. They feel weak and unable to handle or tackle life. Also, they tend to be tactless.

Figure 3.13 shows just a few examples of lip possibilities.

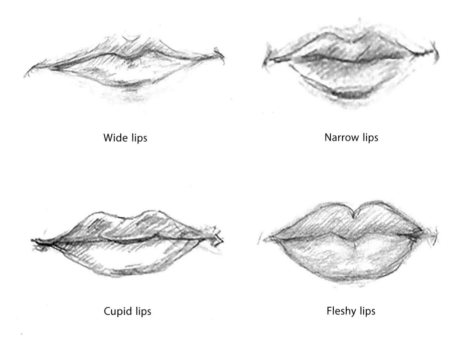

Wide lips   Narrow lips

Cupid lips   Fleshy lips

Fig. 3.13. Lip types: front view

Lips: Cupid

I had another little patient who had beautiful cupid lips, and I said to the mother, "He is very sensitive and somewhat feminine." She said, "Yes, you're absolutely right. He loves wearing my shoes, and he loves wearing lipstick, and all that stuff." Yes, the lips can tell you a lot.

The following lists provide many examples of what the mouth and the lips can reveal in a reading.

Mouth

- A pointed mouth is associated with an adroit charming personality. The whole focus of the mouth comes to the center and forward.
- A wide, long mouth, as seen in Jackie Kennedy and Carol Channing, speaks of avariciousness. When you see a wide mouth, these people are sociable and want power. With a smile they get what they want without exerting much strength. One most often sees a long mouth in children. If that mouth stays long through adult life, it can represent a lack of educability.
- A small mouth indicates a lack of sociability. People with a small mouth are mostly contemplative and have a small group of friends, which they select carefully. You can count on these people.
- A contracted mouth, where the mouth is tight or the lips are pulled in, speaks of people who may be retreating from the world.
- When the mouth moves forward, it can represent sneakiness.
- When the mouth moves backward, it means a lovable, affable nature.
- When the mouth is flat, the person can stand up to the difficulties of life. These people also make good bluffers, and they do not have fear. They believe in themselves, and they can be arrogant.
- A V-shaped mouth, one where the maxilla (upper jaw) is narrow and comes more to a point anteriorly, signifies people who obtain what they want without using strength and who are considered manly.
- A U-shaped mouth, one where the maxilla is rounded, indicates people who have willpower and vigor for glory.
- Those with an open mouth are not well-developed intellectually.

Lips

- When the upper lip advances over the lower lip, look for sexual disturbances. These people may be very concerned with sexual relationships and may boast about them.

- An epicurean lip is seen when the whole mouth moves forward. People with lips like this enjoy the sensual pleasures of eating delicious things. When you see the thick upper lip protruding further forward than the lower lip, that person looks to gain bodily sensation. The epicurean lip, commonly seen in the morphology of the French, includes a slight protrusion of the upper lip with a little crease in the lower part of the philtrum.

Epicurean Lips

One of my patients had a little baby that she brought in for me to see. When I looked at his face I noticed that he had the most beautiful little epicurean lips (forward). So I said to the mother, "This child looks like he is going to truly enjoy and love the deliciousness of the flavors of food." I explained to her that he had an epicurean lip. Two years later she came back into the office with her little boy and said to me, "I remember what you said about his lips, and boy is it ever true. This kid loves all kinds of food!"

- Pursed lips indicate people who want to keep away from social imposition. They want to defend against people.
- A combative lip is one where both upper and lower lips are protruding.
- Large lips and thick lips speak to timidity.
- If the lips are tight and small, you can count on these people. An example of this is Alexander Haig. He is a tough man with thin upper and lower lips, neither of which are showing (see figure 3.14).

Upper Lip

- The upper lip speaks to sex drive. The need is determined by the thickness of the lip. Increased thickness means increased sexual needs. If thinner, the person needs less sex or the sex drive is

Fig. 3.14. Alexander Haig
(Circa 1970, US Army)

diminished. Also, the thinner the upper lip, the less possibility of reproduction.

- When the upper lip is Mercury (thin) or Venus (Cupid), there is great communication. A Venus lip, shaped like Cupid's bow, indicates love and sexuality.
- A full upper lip with a thin lower lip speaks to stinginess.
- A full upper lip with a fat lower lip speaks to generosity.
- Round upper lips are associated with people who will not respect other people's property. They are ambitious and will use other people.
- A straight upper lip indicates a balanced person.
- A curled upper lip represents a person who desires power.
- A backward upper lip means the person is not attracted to the opposite sex. "Backward" means the top lip is curled around the teeth with no lip showing. These people may have had challenges during their youth.
- When the upper lip is forward, it represents aggressiveness and the desire to dominate people.

- A long upper lip means the person is slow in action and reaction and tends to be celibate.
- Those with a short upper lip are rapid reactors and immediately make contact with the opposite sex.
- A mustache covering the upper lip cuts the instinctual zone from the emotional zone and cuts instinct.

Lower Lip

- The lower lip demonstrates control over one's sexual instinct and success in one's chosen field.
- When the lower lip is distorted, whether from birth or by injury, it indicates a change in one's instinctive nature and can reflect disturbances, indigestion, and prostate difficulties.
- If a lower lip is thicker than the upper, the person is a pleasure seeker.
- If one either bites the lower lip or has the lower lip turned in, it shows introversion.
- If the lower lip is forward, people are unhappy.
- The lower lip that protrudes expresses physical needs and a combative spirit. It might also indicate aggressiveness or brutality. If the lip juts out even farther, the person is debased and may exhibit animal-like behavior. A gross projection of the lower lip can indicate sadism.
- A straight lower lip indicates a person who wants to fight.
- A lower lip that goes backward represents people who want to fight and reach their goals. They are not frightened by blood, and they are not scared away.

Efficiency Lines

When one of my female patients came into my office, I could see that on either side of her lips the commissure (the corners of the mouth where the upper and lower lips meet) was extended and tight creating two horizontal lines. I said to her, "You would be the type of person I would hire for my

front desk." And she replied, "I am the main secretary at a big law office."
When you see these lines extending from the commissure of the lips, it
indicates that the individual is a master at executing tasks.

What Teeth Can Tell Us

The teeth can have as many meanings as the mouth and lips. As we know, the teeth have both an upper and lower component. They also follow the rule "as above, so below."

Crooked teeth in an individual can represent emotional imbalance. Following the law of reciprocity, by straightening the teeth with braces, one can make a person's emotional life more clearly directed.

The direction in which the teeth point also helps explain an individual's nature. For example, if the teeth are pointing inward, these people might be gobbling themselves up. In contrast, if a person's teeth are facing outward, as in buckteeth, they may be gobbling up their neighbors, friends, etc.

By looking at the canine teeth, we can understand one's appetite for sex and food. If an individual has especially long canines, they might be gobbling up their partner. So you might see sadistic tendencies or biting or slashing attitudes in someone with long canines. Orthodontia or dental procedures would correct this.

Long Canines and Crooked Teeth

There was a patient of mine who was having difficulty keeping a boyfriend.
She had extremely long canines. Under advisement, she went to the dentist
and had them ground down and now she is married.

Another individual had severely crooked teeth, and he was unable
to get an acting job no matter what he did. He invested in braces, which
changed his whole face, and he got an acting job soon after they came off.
While one might just imagine that straightening the teeth could bring a
more handsome smile, we know from morphology that by straightening
the teeth we straighten our direction in life, as it did in this case.

While dental procedures can certainly redirect one's life for the better, it is interesting to note that in France, face morphology is such a part of the culture that they discourage capping the teeth, because they think it can create an imbalance in and around the muscles of the mouth.

Corrections can be made in ways other than orthodontia; for example, with plastic surgery, acupuncture, mental imagery, and muscle massage. As you will see later, muscle massage can become an accessible and specific tool for working with your own face. Now that you know something about face morphology, when you want to change an aspect of your face, you will be able to exercise the specific muscles needed for the change you desire. This will all become much clearer in the next chapter on muscles.

If a person looks in the mirror and notices that his or her mouth is pointing downward, as in a frown, and they have lines of bitterness that come down off the commissures, we have already seen that the person can literally put a finger on either side of the mouth and push the smile up to make a correction.

Smile Exercise

Here is an exercise to do for twenty-one days. First, put a mirror by the door. Before you exit your home, smile into the mirror and then keep the image of your smiling face with you throughout the day. Second, during your waking day at every chance you have, place your fingers on either side of your mouth by the commissures and lift upward to put your lips into a smile. When you do this every day for twenty-one days, it can bring joy and humor into your life. Consequently, the lines of bitterness will disappear.

There are mental exercises that can be done using the law of reciprocity to change the muscular structure of one's face. By working with the inner self on the inner plane, you can see and experience outer changes. (For instance, using the smile example, breathe out and in three times. See, sense, and feel a happy smile on your face, and then open your eyes.)

Here are some morphological observations about three different dental situations:

1. A gap between the two front teeth represents a disregard for society or an irreverence for authority. When I see the gap, I might say to the person, "Somewhat irreverent, aren't you?" And they give a little giggle of acknowledgment.
2. If one tooth angles backward, it can create dishonesty in the individual, both inwardly toward oneself and outwardly toward others. Orthodontia can help this.
3. If a person loses teeth, it can indicate a health situation. Even dreams of losing teeth could mean an impending health situation. So you want to pay attention to such dreams.

Reading the Chin

In and of itself, the chin means determination. The chin is defined as the area running from the ends of the corner of the mouth to the tip of the bony prominence where the neck meets the face.

The chin is composed of the bone and the muscles that surround the bone. One of the major muscles composing the chin is the mentalis. If the movement of the chin and the mentalis muscle is upward, it speaks to optimism. If the movement of the chin is downward, meaning the mentalis muscle is downward, it represents pessimism. This muscle defines the contour of the chin, whether cleft or ball.

If the chin is pointed, it is considered mercurial and is seen in rapidly acting people with increased power of expression. It is also equivalent to a certain dissipation of energy. Fred Astaire had a pointed chin, and while he was known as a great tap dancer, which meant, in effect, that he was not troubled by a normal dissipation of energy, he was still true to type in that he needed to do short bursts of activity with recovery time. His mercurial chin gave him the speed and intensity that he is famous for, and since a dance lasts only for a limited period of time, he was able to recover as is necessary for mercurial types. Also, his Sun/Jupiter forehead gave him the stick-to-itiveness of the Sun and the visionary aspects of Jupiter. Together these aspects of the forehead gave him the potential to be the creative and dedicated dancer that we know him to be.

A round chin has stability, and a person who possesses this does not impose his or her own will on others.

A square chin represents the power of determination, and a person with such a chin might want to impose his or her will on others and not be considerate of them.

A horizontal line on the chin under the lip shows skepticism or doubt. It is often found in the American culture because we are raised skeptically. The lip turns down, and the more turned down and outward the lip, the more the skepticism is visible.

Even though one can change such a lip in oneself, when you see this lip in another, never try to convince the person of anything that is esoteric unless it is tangible. It is difficult for such people to understand esotericism. They need something tangible to hold on to.

People with a ball-shaped chin consider themselves important, sometimes to an extreme. The ball-shaped chin shows determination and a search for honor and glory.

A short chin looks for more honor in the world and tends to be more organized, while a long-chinned person likes repetitive work. The longer the chin, the greater the lassitude. Stan Laurel had a long chin.

An angle is formed by the base of the chin in relation to the neck. The normal angle is considered to be between 90° and 110° (see figure 3.15). If the angle is less than 90°, also called a negative angle, it is considered an imbalance and may indicate an increased desire for self. An angle greater than 90° is associated with the Lymphatic temperament.

A cleft in the chin has been associated with dishonesty. Yet the

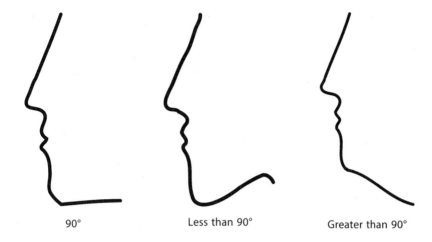

| 90° | Less than 90° | Greater than 90° |

Fig. 3.15. Jaw angles

cleft can cut a person's inclination and make them fight to become more honest. An example of this chin can be seen on Kirk Douglas and many other actors. The acting profession gives people with this chin the opportunity to turn this tendency into art.

A double chin is usually Lymphatic and is what is known as a dewlap. The dewlap is the little bag of flesh at the base of the chin that is seen in the portly and is very common in the Irish, English, and Russians.

Encouragement for People Who
Think They Are Flawed

Oftentimes, when confronted with a dewlap, people—women especially— would like to have it removed, but I counsel them to be careful and not to do it because the dewlap is a reservoir of energy and removing it would cause the person to lose a lot of energy. It's like Dr. Epstein looking at my fat and saying, "Nice library," because the fat, when organized or phlegmatic, holds information. By acknowledging the beneficial aspect of what is usually considered a negative attribute, he brought forward a compassionate quality of face morphology. I like to say to people things like, "Great reservoir of energy." Or "Good stamina in your eyebrows because they are nice and thick. Don't tweeze them." Or "Nice Bilious tip of the nose." I'm just giving people acknowledgment of their positive attributes. If someone comes in with a nose that juts out far from their face, I'll tell them, "I love that nose. It shows me your intelligence."

If only people could see things from this morphological perspective. People look in the mirror and think they are flawed because of standards and ideals that are man-made, and it's a trap. The qualities of some features are amazing. If a person has a nice full philtrum, I'll tell the person, "You must have unending energy!" And they acknowledge it and say that yes, they do. It's wonderful to hear that.

What We Hear from the Ear

The whole external part of the ear is known as the pinna or auricle and it has several parts: the helix, the shell (a.k.a. concha), the lobe (a.k.a. lobule), the antitragus, and the tragus (see facing figure 3.16). The bigger the pinna, the more the intelligence. The more the ears stick out away from the head, the more independent the person is.

Independent Ears

I love the ears, especially the independent ears. When you see the ears really sticking out of the skull, it is a clear indication of independence. I don't usually bring up the issue of dependency when the ears are very close to the head, but when the ears are really sticking out, the independent ears, I feel comfortable speaking about them. For example, when a mother

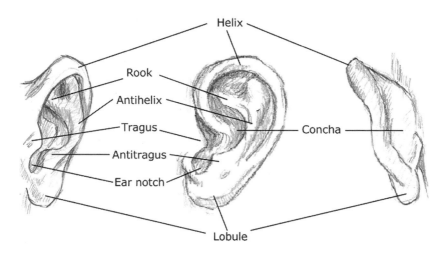

Fig. 3.16. Parts of the exterior ear

comes in and asks about her child, I'll say, "This is going to be a very
independent person." And the mother will say something like "Oh, yeah."
For the child has already demonstrated this independence very early on, at
one, two, or three years old.

The ear is divided into three zones: intelligence, sociability, and the material world. The top or intellectual zone can be as much as half the ear. The middle or sociability zone is up to one-third of the ear, while the lower or material zone can be up to one-fifth of the ear.

If the ear is vertical, it is considered Sanguine; if it slants back, it is considered Nervous. Small-eared people are more influenced by the world. They do not have as much protection. Ears that are pinned back indicate introverted people, while people with ears that jut out are extroverted and mostly independent. For example, excessively large-type ears can be recklessly independent and cannot bear to be controlled at all. Large ears also equal increased strength and the ability to catch the ear of the world—they can hear the world and have the world hear them. Sometimes hiding the ear with the hair can be effective at removing extreme behaviors associated with the ears.

When a person becomes older, you see organic degeneration in the ear. The first sign of this degeneration is that the helix becomes more transparent. When you see that the helix is wrinkly, it can represent dehydration.

A cauliflower (deformed) ear might be found on someone who has been in a fight.

In the shell, or the concha, you see a lot about sociability. The thicker the rim of the shell, the more sociable one is. Also, the larger the shell, the greater the sociability.

The tragus represents energy levels. If you can see the tragus when looking straight on, the person has a high level of energy and vitality. Extroversion is directly proportional to the space between the tragus and antitragus, which helps determine how much one talks as well. The more space, the more talkativeness. The less space, the less talkativeness. Decreased space can also speak to increased paranoia and suspicion.

The lobe speaks to instinctual and material life. A person with a big, thick, hanging lobe has an increased material desire.

A heavy lobe can also indicate an increased equilibrium and therefore inside quiet, and the heavy elongated lobe can be a sign of deep spirituality as is seen in the Buddha. We must be precise when addressing a heavy lobe.

A horizontal lobe, in which the bottom tip faces forward, is seen as sensual, but a possessor of this lobe might also be combative and represent a fighter. If the lobe movement is diagonal, parallel to the movement of the jaw, we see tension and lack of inner control.

People with attached lobes are excellent with money and are practical, but they do not like money. For this reason, they tend to be the best people to ask what to do with your money because they do not like to have it themselves.

Morphology is so revealing that people for generations, especially in show business, have intuitively understood it and usually cast their characters accordingly. One of the exaggerated versions of this was seen with the fictitious characters known as the Ferengi in the Star Trek series *Deep Space Nine*. They were aliens with large ears with attached lobes, and their entire emphasis was on money acquisition. One of the expressions used in the show to determine whether or not one had the ability to acquire money was "He's got the lobes for it."

Ear Tubercle

A mother brought her son in complaining that he had ADHD to such an extent that he was unable to be in the school system because of his behavior issues. Upon observing his profile, I noticed a tubercle on his ear, which can indicate an interference with his behavior. I suggested the ear tubercle could have contributed to his issue. They had the tubercle surgically removed and as of this writing, he has completed two years of college.

The Hair

While each of the four temperament types can have all kinds of hair, as mentioned in previous chapters the hair tends to appear as follows:

- Bilious hair is inclined to be dark, black or brown, thick, and can be straight or curly.
- Nervous hair tends to be light brown and thin.
- Sanguine hair is inclined to be variations of blond or red and can be thick and wavy.
- Lymphatic hair is inclined to be various shades of brown and tends to be fine.

Hair represents strength and sexuality. Factors that affect it are color, thickness, and the amount of curls. The thicker the hair, the greater the strength. The curlier the hair, the greater the sexuality.

General health is fleshed out by hair, nails, and teeth. Similar to what we saw with the teeth, dreams of losing the hair can also indicate an impending health situation. If any of these elements are not growing fully, there could be deficiencies in many ways, but each particular type has a different situation. For example, it is normal for a Moon type to have thin hair because of his or her thyroid. It may not mean the same if, for example, a Bilious type comes in with thin hair, because the Bilious typically have thick, wavy, dark hair that is rich and full.

So to determine if the hair on someone is changing, you have to take into consideration the type. You always want to look at what is in the moment, but if you have an opportunity to see what was (through photos of one sort or another), it will give you an indication of that person's health. Sometimes you can see a driver's license photo that is ten years old, and you can see the change over time. Also, patients often ask if they can bring in a picture of their spouse, and you can see the relationship right there in the pictures. When I work with couples who are having difficulty in their relationship, I educate them as to what their temperaments are. I identify the most outstanding characteristic of their morphology that may be interfering with their relationship and offer a possible corrective intervention.

The Haircut That Saved a Marriage

In one particular instance a couple was having trouble in their marriage, as the man was having affairs. Both he and his wife really wanted to stay together. He had thick, curly, Bilious hair. As an intervention, I suggested he cut his hair short to reduce the multiple antennae of his hair attracting women. And it worked.

When the color of the hair is red, the person is usually a Mars type and can exhibit a fiery temper. Yellow hair that is usually associated with the Sun front-face and is seen on Apollo can have a distancing quality. In the United States, it is an American look to have blond hair, and if it is thick and curly, it increases sexuality.

Thick black hair is associated with the Saturn type and is considered Bilious. This hair quality is often seen in people who dwell on their thoughts and are usually careful. They can also be morose, and in the extreme, they can fall into depression.

Thin hair can represent lack of vigor or strength or both. Mercury/Nervous types tend to have thin, feather-like hair, and in general, brown and blond hair tends to be thinner. Thin hair is also often seen in Jupiter, Neptune, and Moon types, who are Lymphatics. Lymphatics are considered the endocrine type, and as you know, thin hair is associated with hypothyroidism. Given their endodermic nature, they tend to be on the heavy side, and can be pudgy, without overt musculature. They are parasympathetic dominant and can tend to have increased cholesterol levels. This can lead to thinner hair and heavier bodies. We contrast this with Bilious types, who have a strong musculature and on whose head one might see thick and curly hair.

Wavy hair, especially hair that is auburn, is associated with Venus. An actress who was known for her attractive, wavy auburn hair was Rita Hayworth. She had the quintessential aesthetic of an attractive person of her time and was considered a sex symbol, all very fitting for a Venus.

Thick, bushy, steel-wool-like hair in Caucasians speaks to increased sexuality and can be seen in the Saturn and Earth/Bilious types.

Based on the understanding of the law of reciprocity to which we keep returning, you can use hair dye to change the outside to make changes on the inside in the same way that you can use plastic surgery and orthodontia.

Fiery Red Hair

One of my patients had fiery red, curly hair. She was a Mars. She kept complaining that she had knock-down, drag-out fights with her husband and was concerned about her violent nature. In a case like this, the person might be able to quell this nature by dying the hair to mute the fiery redness or by tying it back to make it straight or having it professionally straightened.

How well the hair is kept affects personality. For instance, if the hair goes in many directions, especially on a mate, one might consider the relationship to be troublesome. Since the hair acts as an antenna, curly hair that goes in different directions can receive lots of external impulses, and the individual wearing such a style might be distracted.

It is common for Lymphatic males to grow bald with age. Baldness can also be the consequence of troubled thought. When viewing someone who feels increased tension about business or has trouble in a work relationship, you might observe this kind of baldness.

Facial hair, especially a beard on one who is not a devotee or a religious adept, can be a sign of a cover-up. Of course, fashion and style can counter this observation. Men sometimes hide their chin with a beard if they have a sense that they are not strong enough or masculine enough.

A mustache curtails instinctual life and can even halt its full expression. I was taught that the New York City police department, for example, tends to have many officers with mustaches, perhaps as an unconscious effort to curtail their violent expressions.

Hair covering the forehead can change the expression of the underlying morphology. Conversely, since the forehead is measured from the hairline to the eyebrows, when a person has a receding hairline, it gives the appearance that the forehead is larger than it really is. So, when reading this, try to imagine the hairline pre-balding.

The hairline delineates the shape of the face. When it is smooth and regular, the individual front-face is easier to read and can be considered more accurate to that type. When the hairline is irregular and juts into the forehead at the temporal area, this can indicate a person with many secrets.

4

Reading the
Muscles of the Face

Let's stop for a minute to see where we are and how we got here. We started by looking at the profile, which represents the embryological derivation of the entire individual known as the temperament. The profile is read by observing the structure of the bones and the flesh upon them.

Then we looked at the front-face, which also has bony structures with flesh over them. There are twelve possible front-face shapes. The front-face speaks to personality and character, and it modifies the profile. The individual features then, in turn, modify the front-face. This brings us to the muscles, an important characteristic of the features.

We've already seen that the bony aspects of the face (see figure 4.1 on the next page) are fixed. Short of fracture or surgery, your jaw, your forehead, and the bone of your nose are yours for life. The muscles, on the other hand, can change, and by doing so, as we've seen through the law of reciprocity, can alter your inner state. Figure 4.2 on page 143 shows the muscles that overlie the cranial and facial bones, and it is these muscles that will be discussed in this chapter.

Facial Muscles and Mental Significance

The table beginning on page 144 lists the names of the muscles (along with their corresponding numbers in figure 4.2), their physical

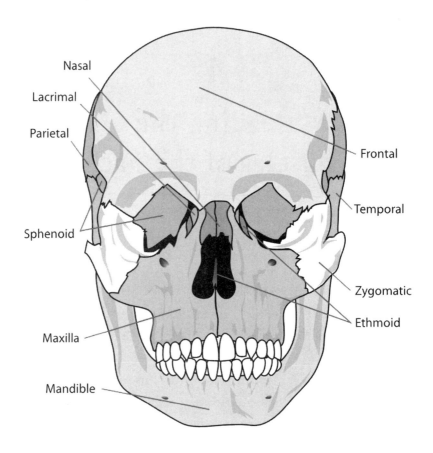

Fig. 4.1. Facial and cranial bones

function, and their mental significance. While some of the names may differ somewhat from those in various anatomy books, they should be identifiable nevertheless.

A person demonstrates the mental characteristics listed in the table when the given muscle is stimulated. If the muscle is neutral, it is considered balanced and the mental characteristics do not apply. Our thoughts manifest in our facial muscles. A muscle that is exercised, or contracted frequently, develops a distinctive tonicity that allows us to read it and see that the person has these mental tendencies.

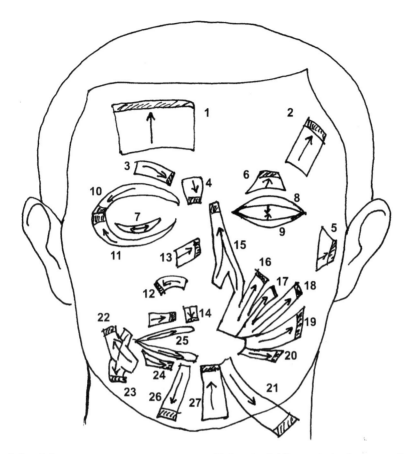

1. Frontalis
2. External frontalis
3. Corrugator supercilii
4. Depressor supercilii (vertical)
5. Auricularis posterior (behind the ear)
6. Levator palpebrae superioris
7. Pretarsalis
8. Superior tarsal
9. Inferior tarsal
10. Orbicularis oculus
11. Preseptalis (preseptal orbicularis)
12. Dilator naris
13. Compressor naris
14. Depressor septi
15. Levator labii superioris alaeque nasi
16. Levator labii superioris (infraorbital head)
17. Zygomaticus minor (zygomatic head of levator labii superioris)
18. Zygomaticus major
19. Buccinator
20. Risorius
21. Platysma
22. Caninus (levator anguli oris)
23. Triangularis (depressor anguli oris)
24. Incisivus
25. Orbicularis oris
26. Quadratus (depressor labii inferioris)
27. Mentalis

Fig. 4.2. Facial muscles
(Adapted from a handout from my course of study
with Dr. Gerald Epstein)

FACIAL MUSCLES

Muscle Name	Physical Function	Mental Significance
Frontalis (1)	Raises the eyebrows and the space between the eyebrows and forms the horizontal furrows across the forehead. If one side alone is activated, it arches the eyebrow while raising it. However, if the external frontalis and the corrugator supercilii are enacted, then the eyebrow stays straight.	Indicates a person who is impressionable.
External frontalis (2)	Formed by the fibers on the outside of the frontal muscle. Elevates the part that is external in the front and forms the lines on the lateral forehead.	Indicates a gesture of surprise and, by extension, an intellectual curiosity, and is found in savants, inventors, and creative people.
Corrugator supercilii (3)	Very small muscle, flattened and spindly, extending the length of the internal part of the arch of the eyebrow. It bulges the head of the eyebrows, drawing the brows together and producing two vertical ridges, sometimes very deep, between them.	One who is attentive and ready to react to their impressions. This can add to their impulsiveness, when they have it, and also to their worry and anxiety.
Depressor supercilii (vertical) (4)	Very thin and very short vertical muscle behind the space between the eyebrows, above the root of the nose. It lowers the space between the eyebrows and the head of the eyebrows, without causing a bulge. It causes one or two horizontal ridges at the level of the root of the nose below the space between the eyebrows.	Indicates one who is obstinate, tenacious, sticks to their ideas, sometimes stubborn.
Auricularis posterior (5)	Retracts ear and brings the pinna closer to the cranium.	Dependency

Muscle Name	Physical Function	Mental Significance
:vator palpebrae perioris)	Makes the upper eyelid go up and back without affecting the lower lid.	If weak, the upper eyelid drops over the iris creating the look of "shifty eyes," a sign of physical or moral release or a loss of restraint. In a very strong contraction, the eyelid exposes a thin white sclerotic band. This muscle can create a sparkly gaze when contracted, but at times, and especially when it is lax, it can be indicative of a sickly state.
etarsalis)	Large, flat muscle below the lower eyelid, right under the eye. Gives the horizontal fold of skin to the eyelid and allows the eyelid to open.	One who has joie de vivre. If this muscle is not engaged, joy is not genuine and a smile or laughter is feigned.
rsal (superior d inferior) and 9)	Small muscle on tarsal cartilage, or eyelid, that closes the eye and allows blinking.	Instinctive adaptation. Part of the body's fight-or-flight response: the bigger the blink, the bigger the surprise. One who is immature emotively: wide-eyed, bright-eyed, bushy-tailed, and naive. Squinting eyes: limited attention, retreat into themselves, do not want people looking into them.
rbicularis oculus 0)	Flat, large orbital muscle with a rectilinear fold that encloses the external commissure of the eye; closes the eye.	Any change in the morphology or function of the muscle indicates one who is much absorbed or concentrating on feelings or actions.

FACIAL MUSCLES (continued)

Muscle Name	Physical Function	Mental Significance
Preseptalis (11)	Large, flat muscle close to the lower orbit. Used in voluntary closing of the eye but more involved in involuntary blinking. Also keeps the eye closed during sleep. Contraction of this muscle can create bags under the eyes, not to be confused with fatty deposits or puffiness due to kidney disorder.	Shows depression or physical tiredness. May indicate insomnia, gastric digestive disturbance, immune depression, or introversion.
Dilator naris (12)	Enlarges nasal aperture. Increases the diameter of the nares.	Indicates sensory desire, sensation with others, love, smell, and taste. Associated with the ability to wait (thin nostrils = not easy to wait).
Compressor naris (13)	Draws alae of nose toward septum, compresses nostrils.	Internal tension, can't relax.
Depressor septi (14)	Pulls nose and upper lip down, making the upper lip puff up.	Indicates opposition, contradiction, and pride.
Levator labii superioris alaeque nasi (15)	Raises the alae (wings) of the nose and makes creases in the nose. Creates nasolabial straight-down-going folds. When things smell bad, we use this muscle.	Allows one to see weak points in others and perceive what is disagreeable, difficult, and annoying about persons or situations. Therefore, these nasal creases may speak to increased pessimism and diminished optimism.
Levator labii superioris (infraorbital head) (16)	Lifts the upper lip, which is a way to look aggressive or offensive.	One who pushes away what is unpleasant or offensive or perceives an obstacle and rejects it.
Zygomaticus minor (zygomatic head of levator lavii superioris) (17)	Lifts the upper lip slightly, lateral to the levator labii superioris (infraorbital head), creating a curved nasolabial fold.	Perceiving moral or psychic pain.

Muscle Name	Physical Function	Mental Significance
zygomaticus major (18)	Lifts the corners of the mouth, more lateral than the zygomaticus minor, as on an open, optimistic smile.	Feeling pleasure that is moral and attached to a feeling, not a sensation (smile of the upper lip is associated with feeling); optimism.
buccinator (19)	Lifts the corners of the mouth but less vertically than zygomaticus major (which runs more vertically upward) and more horizontally to the sides.	Feeling pleasure that is connected more with a sensation than a feeling, more toward things than people (smile of the lower lip is associated with sensation).
risorius (20)	Pulls corners of the mouth nearly straight to the sides, horizontally.	Shows executive ability, independence, and objectivity and one who takes pleasure in autonomous work (without external pressure).
platysma (21)	Pulls corners of the mouth, cheeks, and skin of the neck down and slightly out to the sides.	Recognition of difficult situations and knowing how to take them into account rather than jumping into action.
caninus (levator anguli oris) (22)	Pulls corners of the mouth up in such a way that a "bow tie" or an "olive" shape is created at the corners of the mouth, slightly lifting the upper lip to expose the canine teeth.	Indicates contentment with oneself and pride.
triangularis depressor anguli oris) (23)	The muscle of pessimism. Brings corners of the mouth almost straight down.	Represents bitterness and resentment, painful past experiences, perception of what is unfortunate, and/or experiences of depression.
incisivus (24)	This is a set of paired muscles, one on each side of the upper lip, and one on each side of the lower lip. They pull the upper and lower lips toward the center, as if making a sucking gesture (as in a baby attempting to latch onto a breast), exposing incisor teeth.	Indicates dependence—is appealing but when in a smile indicates a lack of autonomy and the need for others, and desire. When in a smile and seen with zygomaticus major, it means elective attachment with affectionate sociability.

FACIAL MUSCLES *(continued)*

Muscle Name	Physical Function	Mental Significance
Orbicularis oris (25)	A circular muscle that runs around the lips, divided into two in the lower lip and two in the upper lip, as it closes the mouth. Compresses lips together and turns lips inward, or brings the two commissures together ready for a kiss.	Compressing the lips is a defensive movement, closing one from external influences. Indicates not being able or not wanting to accept the system of thinking of others and a tendency to filter outside input to protect oneself. The blowing or kissing posture is equivalent to desire. It can also indicate people recalling their childhood or be seen as derogatory, as in aggressive flirtation.
Quadratus (depressor labii inferioris) (26)	Muscle that brings down corners of the chin, making it look square by contracting inferiorly.	General life-force, energy, vitality, strength, and willfulness.
Mentalis (27)	Muscle that pulls up the center of the chin, creating a ridge on the chin and eventually a horizontal wrinkle. Also lowers the lower lip and provokes advancement of the lower lip out.	Suspending action due to doubt of oneself and others, indecisiveness, and fear of taking action or delegating it. If it's on a strong, energetic face, it may mean maturity and not giving in to impulse.

Practical Application of Reading the Facial Muscles

The table of the muscles above will probably be of most value to you as a reference, but now we need to look at the muscles in greater detail, because this is where we have the ability to work with our understanding of face morphology, not only to read the face but to actually make a change.

I'd first like to express my gratitude to Dr. Oleg Reznik for so generously sharing with me photos he took of himself that demonstrate the facial muscles. These photos inspired me to ask my son, Daniel, to do the same so that I could share his photos with you to further your understanding of how the muscles influence the structure of the face. The photos on pages 150–53 correlate to the muscles of the mouth, which are muscles 14–27 in figure 4.2 and the Facial Muscles table, and the following text will further highlight what some of these muscles can tell us about one's personality.

In the infraorbital head and the alaeque nasi portions of the levator labii superioris, one can see the liver. The infraorbital head of this muscle has an ability to raise and make an arch of the medial lip to show the canine tooth while making the tip of the nose round and dip down. People who exaggerate this particular muscle might have an offensive attitude toward the world. They see obstacles and reject them.

The zygomaticus major muscle is formed from the malar bone at the corner of the lip, and it crosses the buccinator muscle, a deep part of the cheek between the lip commissure and the mandible, making the commissure go up and producing a smile or laugh that indicates moral pleasure. Moral pleasure, it is worth noting, is attached to a feeling of virtue and not sensation, which is a physical perception.

The buccinator is flat, makes a curve, and pushes the lower lip up with a broadening of the buccal cavity creating or causing an upward curl of the smile that represents physical pleasure.

The risorius is the outer commissure of the lip. The median cheek attaches to the masseter and stretches to close the buccal cavity, making a long tight lip and the horizontal lines of the commissure. People with this mouth shape can execute wisely and well, and they are independent and are able to be objective.

The caninus muscle is a four-part muscle from the canine cavity to the maxillary bone to the upper lip. Contractions raise the lower lip commissure and form a structure that gives the impression of an olive. You can see a little ball above the corner of the upper lip. When you observe that olive, it usually connotes pride and conceit.

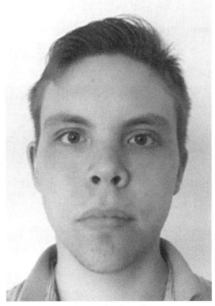

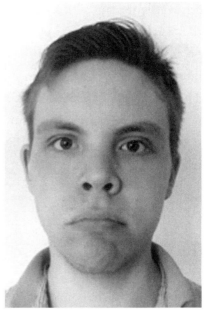

Neutral relaxed

Depressor septi (14)

Levator labii superioris
alaeque nasi (15)

Levator labii superioris (16)

Fig. 4.3. Photos of facial muscles around the mouth

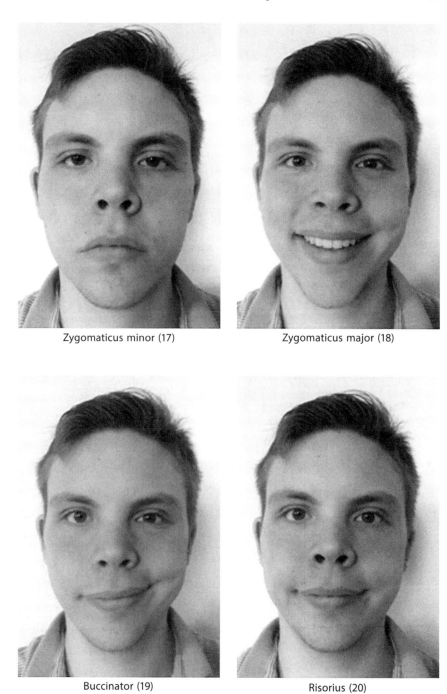

Zygomaticus minor (17)   Zygomaticus major (18)

Buccinator (19)   Risorius (20)

Fig. 4.3. Photos of facial muscles around the mouth *(continued)*

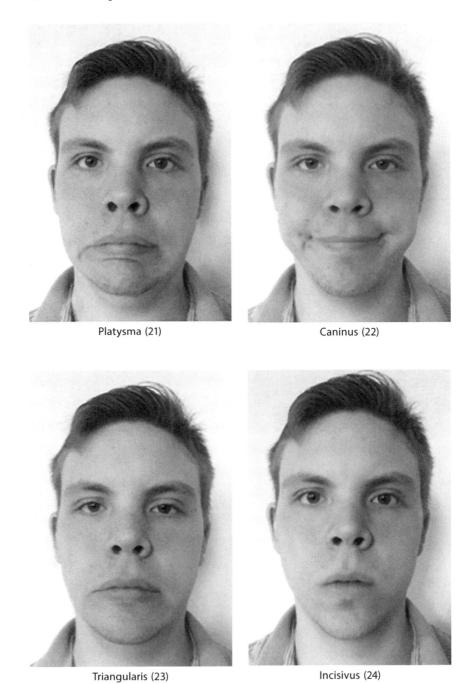

Platysma (21)

Caninus (22)

Triangularis (23)

Incisivus (24)

Fig. 4.3. Photos of facial muscles around the mouth *(continued)*

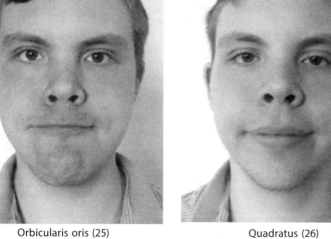

Orbicularis oris (25)   Quadratus (26)

Mentalis (27)

Fig. 4.3. Photos of facial muscles around the mouth *(continued)*

The triangularis muscle fits from the lower maxilla to underneath the mandible. It is a large, thin, flat muscle on the lower jaw connected to the commissure. It pulls the commissure down and out, usually in an expression of pessimism, and has to do with a painful experience, recent or remote. To alter this, massage the buccinator muscle and the zygomaticus major, and see if the person has a change. When you see the triangularis muscle contracted, the person is experiencing a sensation of pain.

Subjectively, it is easy to assess pain in another whether it is physical or emotional, and the face often reveals that pain.

The orbicularis oris gives the appearance of a muscle surrounding the mouth. When that muscle is large, the person must come to terms with the tendency to use one's charm for deceit. The internal portion of this muscle contains two symmetrical parts. As a result, you see the thickness of both the upper lip and the commissure, and you see the lower lip close. This closing action will block external influences. It is a defensive posture. By closing the mouth this way, the lips are inside (as seen in photo of orbicularis oris above). When you see this posture, do not waste time trying to get through to the person. There are four external parts to this muscle, two in the lower lip and two in the upper lip. These muscles bring the two commissures together, ready for a kiss. The blowing or kissing posture is equivalent to desire. This can be observed culturally in Frenchmen, and coincidently, they have a reputation for being pensive about the opposite sex. We are familiar with this facial posture in Maurice Chevalier.

The mentalis muscle raises the chin and lowers and provokes an outward advancement of the lower lip. It is usually seen when one is doubting oneself or possibly doubting everything. You might notice a crease underneath the lower lip, which is evidence of habitual use of this muscle. When this is observed, it can indicate a chronic lack of self-confidence. A person with this posture cannot delegate authority easily.

As we have already described the lips, we have a good understanding of one's relationship to the world regarding the upper and lower lips. The muscles surrounding the mouth can alter the holding of the lips. While we understand that one may inherit the thickness and thinness of the lips, the muscles support this, and you may notice that people can posture their lips in such a way as to accentuate or diminish their disposition.

It is also interesting to note that in addition to understanding that morphology can reveal personality and an individual's personal tendencies, we also know that certain aspects of the face relate to organs. For instance, the tissue of the lip relates to the sexual organs, with the upper lip crease relating more specifically to the genitals. The upper tissue of the lip relates to the stomach. The lower lip represents the large intestine, the kidney, and in men, the prostate. The medial cheek relates to the lung.

Muscles That Indicate
Particular States of Mind

The information in the following tables was translated, abbreviated, and organized from material taught in Dr. Epstein's classes and in the book *Connaitre les autres par: le visage,* by Jean Gaussin. This book references research performed by Henri Rouvière, appearing in his book *Anatomie humaine: descriptive et topographique,* involving electric stimulation of facial muscles to illicit the sentiment associated with the corresponding muscles as listed in the tables below. It is clear that the facial muscles create the emotions, feelings, and mental states consistently. Each muscle creates the same feeling in all people. Practitioners who are familiar with acupuncture or who practice kinesiology may be able to help people by strengthening the muscle that creates the desired feeling, emotion, or mental construct.

MUSCLES INDICATING JOY

Muscle	Indication
Pretarsalis (7)	Enthusiasm
Dilator naris (12)	Desire
Zygomaticus major (18)	Pleasure
Buccinator (19)	Pleasure of the senses
Risorius (20)	Joy of action

MUSCLES INDICATING SADNESS

Muscle	Indication
Depressor supercilii (vertical) (4)	Stubbornness
Levator palpebrae superioris (6)	Stopping
Orbicularis oculus (10)	Preoccupation
Preseptalis (11)	Physical lassitude
Compressor naris (13)	Tension
Zygomaticus minor (17)	Psychic suffering
Triangularis (23)	Disillusion
Mentalis (27)	Doubt

MUSCLES INDICATING EFFICACY OR EFFICIENCY

Muscle	Indication
Depressor supercilii (vertical) (4)	Obstinacy
Orbicularis oculus (10)	Concentration
Preseptalis (11)	Measure
Compressor naris (13)	Stiffening
Zygomaticus minor (17)	Protection
Platysma (21)	Maturity
Triangularis (23)	Forecasting
Mentalis (27)	Doubt

MUSCLES INDICATING AUTHORITY

Muscle	Indication
Depressor septi (14)	Opposition
Levator labii superioris alaeque nasi (15)	Displeasure
Levator labii superioris (infraorbital head) (16)	Offensiveness
Caninus (22)	Pride
Orbicularis oris (25)	Defensiveness

Teaching Experience

I used to teach classes in religious instruction for confirmation students. In trying to explain to them the sentiment of the Holy Spirit, I had them each sit across from each other and try to recollect a time in their life that was either auspicious or outstanding in some way. As one person contemplated an event, I asked the other person to try to change their face, gestures, and body posture to mimic the other person and see if it elicited a response in them. Each and every one of the students was able to identify what that other person was thinking and feeling without language, by simply imitating their posture.

5

Applying the Knowledge of Temperament beyond the Face

You will recall that the features modify the front-face and the front-face modifies the temperament. These three levels of structure in the face come together in endless possible combinations, making each of us unique. Now that you understand these three levels, we will consider some additional temperament-related aspects, many of which go beyond the face.

Temperament Indications of the Body

We've already seen that we can get confirming information from the structures of the face, but there are other physical characteristics that can provide us with additional clues to a person's temperament, personality, and overall identity, such as palm color, body posture, and voice quality.

Palm Color

Often we notice that people tend to put their best face forward, and we might assume them to be what they appear to be. However, simultaneously, there could be an inner feeling or nature that they might want to hide, and people will often use makeup and even surgery to cover up their natural morphology. So when reading the face, we will also want to look at the color of the palm of the hand to see if the complexion of the palm is the same as or different from the complexion of the face. Since the palm color is hidden from the elements of nature, is not always seen by others, and is rarely, if ever, disguised by makeup, it may be a truer revealer of temperament.

The colors of the palm associated with the different temperaments are as follows: black/Bilious, yellow/Nervous, red/Sanguine, and white/Lymphatic.

The Morphology of Body Postures

While in this book we are primarily concentrating on the face, many of us know that there is something called "body language" that enables practitioners to read the meaning of their clients' or patients' body positions, both negative and positive. Chiropractors are trained to assess posture, from the most intuitive impression of a handshake (because of its muscular tone or intensity) to the more subtle implication of the way people walk or the way they hold their body. We notice things like whether the shoulders are slumped or upright or are held forward or in a "green light" posture—always leaning forward trying to get to something quickly.

These postural observations can also be included in the study of morphology. If there is hesitancy in a client's posture, it tells us that he does not want to face the world. If a client's head is down, it tells us that it is difficult for her to see where she is going in life. Sometimes there is a deliberate outward thrusting of the chin. This thrusting especially can occur in men who have a weak chin—they intuitively lift their chin outward to make themselves feel stronger.

These body postures are elements of the morphological system. When people understand the inherent inclinations in their body postures and gestures, they can try to compensate for these meanings through their musculature.

The classic reading of the face also includes understanding gestures and evaluating balance. However, if you learn the rules of morphology, you will also come to know what structural, physical changes mean when you observe them.

Voice Associated with Planetary Face Shapes

The voice is considered a secondary sex characteristic and is the portrayal of hormonal functioning. It can also be used in addition to fingerprints, palm prints, and face morphology to identify an individual.

While the timbre of the voice can be categorized and described in the context of the front-face shapes, we should also understand that the tone, intensity, and clarity of the voice have characteristics as well.

For example, one can assess the intensity of the voice. If a person is sick and the health is failing, or if a person has just recovered from illness and/or surgery, you might notice that the voice is thinner, higher, and less resonant. On the other hand, you might have in your life people who have booming voices. Without effort, they sound like they are yelling or shouting, and you might notice that they are excessive in all areas of their lives. Or if a person who normally has a deep, booming voice suddenly has a voice that is higher than usual and not as loud, one might consider that there is an underlying health problem and pay attention to that.

Now let's consider the voice qualities of the planetary face shapes as shown in the list below.

- **Saturn voice:** low pitched and turned in, as if the person does not truly want to be heard
- **Earth voice:** short or clipped speech, fitting the sharpness and desire of the Earth type to overpower
- **Uranus voice:** resonates more in the head rather than project-

ing outward—and cutting, as is heard in Edward R. Murrow's voice

- **Mercury voice:** light, captivating, and charming, which is in accord with the characteristics of a Mercury front-face personality—they tend to be performers
- **Mars voice:** piercing, perforating, and sheer, which fits the aggressive personality that is associated with the Mars front-face
- **Pluto voice:** strong like the Mars voice
- **Venus voice:** lilting and musical, which is analogous to the feminine and attractive personality associated with Venus
- **Sun voice:** resonant and distant at the same time, with a far-away quality
- **Jupiter voice:** naturally deep and can be booming
- **Moon voice:** thin with no vibrato
- **Neptune voice:** like the Mercury voice but deeper

Evaluation and Supplementation by Temperament

As we start this next topic, we cover many subjects that are basic to the task of reading the morphology such as diagnosing and supplementing by considering the four temperaments and their embryological derivation.

Using Temperament Types to Evaluate Patients by Proclivity

We know now that when we encounter a person with a particular symptom or issue, we should look at their primary embryological derivation.

For instance, although Bilious types, who are derived from the chordoblast layer, are typically healthy overall, they can still have issues with the ligaments, tendons, liver, gallbladder, and, especially in the Saturn front-face type, bones.

Nervous types, derived from the ectoderm layer, can have

neurological dysfunctions, are prone toward emotional lability, and have the shortest digestive tract. They are also disposed to a nervous stomach and can have skin disorders.

The Sanguine, whose temperament is derived from the mesoderm layer, can have problems in the cardiovascular system and heart muscle. If they are a Venus Sanguine, we must also concentrate on the reproductive area.

Lymphatic types, because they are derived from the endoderm layer, are prone to endocrine dysfunction and a capacity to overindulge, so we must always consider problems like diabetes, thyroid dysfunction, pancreas disorders, and gallbladder issues.

Here are some examples of where you can see the benefit of face morphology in assessing the organs of the body for each of the temperaments.

Bilious Digestive Distress

A patient who was a Caucasian woman with a Bilious temperament came into the office saying she had had gastric distress for a very long time. She'd been to every single kind of clinic and doctor to be evaluated, but they had brought her no relief. I looked at her and noticed that her skin was mildly jaundiced—or yellow—which is usually the Nervous temperament's color, not the Bilious's. This morphological clue led me to further investigate through other natural and noninvasive methods, which caused me to suspect that a particular African parasite might be the cause of her distress. Not wanting to plant this idea in her head, I simply asked her if she had traveled recently. When she said no, I asked if she had any relationship to Africa, and she said, "My husband is African."

It turned out that she had a condition called bilharziasis, which was caused by a liver fluke that had settled in various organs of her abdomen, primarily in her liver, and was creating sickness. Because she was Caucasian, the other healthcare practitioners were not looking for an African disease.

Nervous Digestive Distress

A petite patient with a Nervous temperament came into the office saying that she had been diagnosed with spastic colon and was seeking nutritional help. Knowing that those of the Nervous temperament have the shortest digestive tract and are the true vegetarians, I suggested that she eat less meat and try a more vegetable-based diet. She did so, and her colon responded nicely.

Evaluating a Headache

- If it is a Bilious who comes in with a headache, we should look at the liver and gallbladder for the dysfunction.
- If it is a Nervous with a headache, we must look at the brain.
- If it is a Sanguine with a headache, then we have to consider the cardiovascular system.
- If it is a Lymphatic with a headache, we must look for endocrine dysfunction.

Sanguine Headache

A patient came into the office with a blaring headache and upon looking at her morphology, I could see she was a Sanguine. She stated that she was just looking for a "crack" because another chiropractor had helped her with her headaches by osseously adjusting her. She heard about me and really wanted to see what I could do.

Her headache was very severe, and since she was a Sanguine, I was quite concerned. So I did some neurological diagnostic tests in my office and then immediately sent her to the hospital and asked them to do a spinal tap. It turned out that she had a subarachnoid bleed—a slow bleed in her brain—and within ten days she could have been dead. The doctors called me back and thanked me because she had been in the emergency room several days before, and they had sent her home saying she just had a headache.

Lymphatic Headache

A young man came into the office with severe headaches. While he was not overly fat or overweight, he had the Lymphatic temperament. Everyone was trying to evaluate him for migraines and looking at the cardiovascular system, but for some reason his headaches always went away when people wanted to examine him. Since he was Lymphatic, I questioned him regarding his endocrine history, and it turned out that his headaches occurred after lovemaking. I referred him to an endocrinologist who confirmed that when this patient had sex his hormone levels became irregular and caused cluster headaches.

Supplemental Support and Contraindications Associated with the Temperament Types

You will see in the following examples that vitamins and nutritional supplements can sometimes be hazardous when one does not understand the morphological type receiving them.

Bilious types, deriving from the chordoblast, can use calcium to help the difficulties that they can have with tendons and bones. In contrast, even though they can have brittle bones, people with the Nervous temperament, which derives from ectoderm, react poorly to calcium. They do better with boron.

Excessive vitamin C is not good for Nervous types because it leads to an increased pumping of the stomach juices, and the ascorbic acid can irritate the stomach lining. In addition, Nervous types are sympathetic rather than parasympathetic, and vitamin C in sympathetic types interacts poorly with the pepsinogen in the stomach. However, there are other vitamins that can support these ectoderms. One of them is thiamin hydrochloride, or vitamin B₁, which can soothe Nervous types.

Understanding that the mesoderm gives rise to the adrenals, we would want to use vitamin C if we choose to supplement the diet of a Sanguine. A Lymphatic, however, derives from endoderm, therefore vitamin C might not be a good choice for that type.

Digestion and Temperament

If you know the temperament, you know the length of the person's digestive tract, which determines the kinds of foods that person would do well to eat. With this simple evaluation of the profile, you can council a person on the percentages of foods that will help them thrive, whether meats, vegetables, or grains. Here is a review and summary of the basic digestive characteristics of each temperament.

Bilious Digestion

The digestive tract of the Bilious is medium in length and does well with the Mediterranean diet, which offers a moderate amount of protein. The Bilious need a good deal of oxygenation. While they are omnivores, they do well to protect themselves by reducing their intake of red meat, poultry, lamb, and root vegetables. They need a lot of ozone, and they do best by eating fish, grain, and leafy green vegetables—foods that are rich in oxygen.

Nervous Digestion

The Nervous type is the true vegetarian due to their short digestive tract. It is difficult for them to be comfortable eating large amounts of protein. They need to eat six to eight times per day in small amounts. The longer the gastrointestinal tract, the longer the food is kept in the gut. Since the Nervous digestive tract is shorter, this type needs lighter foods.

Sanguine Digestion

The Sanguine has the second longest digestive tract and does very well on three square meals a day. They enjoy large amounts of protein. They need the flesh to make muscle and tend to be quite muscular. They use moderate amounts of liquid and small amounts of vegetables and fruits. They need large amounts of protein and do well eating three times per day, but not between meals. Most Sanguines admit that they enjoy eating meat.

Lymphatic Digestion

The Lymphatic has the longest digestive tract and can eat anything. They also tend to overeat. They are truly the digestive type, meaning they digest concepts and information as well as food.

Temperament Type: Pure or Mixed?

In America we truly are a conglomerate of many nations, and therefore our faces are not considered pure. Instead, they can be a mix of temperaments and planetary front-faces with all the nuances that go along with them. Other cultures or countries, though, may be easier to type since they do not mix and mingle as much.

Cultural Proclivities

Since many cultures and countries have less intermarriage than America, we might be able to characterize a whole country as a particular type. For example, the French tend to be Nervous types, while Russians tend to be Lymphatics, Italians tend to be Bilious, and the English tend to be Sanguine or Lymphatic.

Also, you might see typical front-face characteristics in these cultures. For example, Italians as well as Israelis can have the Moon or Venus front-face, while Germans tend to have Mars front-faces with Sanguine profiles.

In addition, environmental factors can change the physiology and look of people. A generalization is that people living in the northern regions are taller, while in the southern regions they are shorter. Northern people tend to be more dominant in the world, since there is a perception that the taller the person, the more dominant they are; however, there is a compensatory dominance in short people in trying to compete with people of height.

Planetary Front-Face Combinations

As mentioned above, we are in a society where there is a lot of mixing, and the different face possibilities are endless. Once we become acclimated to the qualities and characteristics associated with each of the planetary front-face shapes, we can note that a face may have part this shape and part that. For instance, someone may have a Mars face but Moon quality eyes and nose, and that is going to change the intensity of the Mars. Or one might see a Venus forehead with a strong-angled Pluto jaw.

All of these combinations can be read with experience. By acknowledging the characteristic attributes and inclinations of each of the planetary types and superimposing them over each other, you will gain an understanding of the nuances they generate. Remember, though, that morphology is a science that is spoken to from your initial, intuitive hit, as well as from your heart, so you will see the primary type in your first initial glance, and you are encouraged to trust that.

Here are some examples of front-face combinations that you might see:

- When the left eye is Moon-shaped (round), and the right eye is Sun-shaped (almond), it may indicate that a person is psychic or highly sensitive, while the reverse—the left eye is Sun while the right eye is Moon—may indicate mental confusion.

> It is accepted in morphology that the right side of the body represents the male aspect of the self, and the left side of the body represents the female aspect of the self.

- Mars over Saturn is one who may plot revenge.
- Lymphatic types with a Jupiter forehead are considered visionaries. They see the broader picture and tend not to be interested in details. They see the ramifications of people's thoughts and actions.

- A man with a combination of Mars and Sun can be a womanizer.
- Moon upper lip over Mars lower lip tends to prevaricate.
- Occasionally you may see a Saturn over a Sun type. This may create difficulty for the individual as Saturn types have trouble showing outward expression, while the Sun type shows outward expression easily.

Back of the Head: A Combination Profile

I had a patient who had the most extraordinary bullet shape on the back of the head, but on the profile he did not appear to be a Nervous temperament as much as a Sanguine. So if I had limited my evaluation to the forehead and jaw, I would have concluded that this was a simple Sanguine. But the bullet head clued me in to an important aspect of this person's temperament that was very revealing. As I spoke with the patient, I realized that given his quickness and wit and the speed with which he spoke, he actually was a Nervous type. I knew this because Nervous temperaments have the most wonderful ability to speak. The most interesting thing about this person was that he was bouncing between the Nervous and Sanguine temperaments. So even though the jaw did not match the bullet head, the bullet head was revealing that there was an underlying Nervous component.

Relationships

Which temperaments go well together?

I often heard Dr. Gerald Epstein tell the story of how his teacher Colette, with her mastery of morphology, looked at the back of the head of a man and said he was going to be her husband. She could see his entire essence in the back of his head. Here is the story as I remember it.

Colette saw that this particular man had a spatulated back of the head. This meant he was a Sanguine and as such had to be on the move all the time. He would constantly be working at something and using his hands. He would be the one to shop for food, serve the people, and clear the table. She knew he would be the perfect mate for her, as he would take care of these matters and leave her free to concentrate on her teaching. And he was; so they married.

Some temperaments go well together, and some do not. Here's a rundown of possibilities.

Two Lymphatics go well together. Both are placid and tranquil, indulge in food, enjoy going places together, and enjoy companionship.

Bilious and Lymphatic also go together well. Bilious types are very outgoing and like to have their will met. The Lymphatic type does not mind complying. In fact, Lymphatics are very easy-going and welcome meeting the will of the Bilious temperament. Lymphatics feel that they are protected by the Bilious strength of will.

Sanguine and Nervous do well together, too. Sanguine strength makes the Nervous feel protected. Nervous types tend to think the ground is crumbling under their feet. They are always jittery, so they do not feel stable on the earth. Meanwhile, the Sanguine enjoy the great élan and quickness, fun, and humor of Nervous types.

Bilious and Nervous do not go well together, because the will of the Bilious needs to be met, and the Nervous type wants its needs to be met first. Saying "the will of the Bilious needs to be met" means the Bilious have to be given to first. The Nervous type disagrees and (internally and probably unconsciously) says, "No, first give to me, because as you give to me, and you draw me in, you will be showing your adulation and applause. That then stimulates me to want to respond and reciprocate." But this is not going to happen.

Bilious and Sanguine also do not go well together in an intimate relationship, but they go together very well as a team in public enterprise because they both have active qualities and the capacity to be strong together in these situations. But Sanguines, who tend to be great salespeople, can be forceful and dominant. In intimate relationships, the tenacious or controlling will of the Bilious clashes with the soldier-like will of the Sanguine, who is stubborn and obstinate and not going to be pushed off the dime, so to speak. They will not be pushed around. The two temperaments can come into great conflict with each other.

Sanguine and Lymphatic are not compatible either. The Sanguine is too active for the Lymphatic who wants to be passive and is not interested in the same level of physical activity (except for swimming or walking). Lymphatic types are visionaries. They see things in their minds and have great ideas. Sanguine types in contrast become bored by prolonged conversation and have a short attention span. They do not want to listen to visionary ideas. When they are not active, they repose without thought.

Nervous and Lymphatic do not do well together for a simple reason: Who is going to take out the garbage? They are both passive types, and it is not in their nature to be first initiators, so they become exasperated with each other. However, they are both cerebral and can work together in that way. Lymphatic types like to synthesize ideas. This combination may enjoy sharing arts and movies together, but ultimately, Nervous and Lymphatic types do not feel protected by each other, and this can create a problem in the relationship.

As Dr. Epstein always taught, you get the most out of a relationship when both parties are the same or 180 degrees opposite. That usually affords the soul the most learning. In keeping with that, a **Bilious/Bilious** relationship, being the same, can be quite fortuitous. However, the Bilious's need to dominate may cause them to butt heads. The **Nervous/Nervous** relationship, in the same way, can be very satisfying on the intellective plane. However, the fears and anxieties about health, and the passivity of the Nervous nature, can prove difficult in their relationship. The **Sanguine/Sanguine** relationship, while in the physical arena is a match made in heaven, given the analytical nature of each of them, may create a conflict in who is right. Also, due to their excessive nature, there is no one there to curb their overuse of substance. As mentioned at the beginning of this section, the **Lymphatic/Lymphatic** relationship is generally an enjoyable one.

As you can imagine, there are many combinations of temperament that have been forming relationships for eternity, and all of the qualifiers of that temperament, including one's will, can make or break the couple.

Conclusion

You now know how to read the profile, the front-face, the features, and the muscles, and you have an idea of how to help yourself, your loved ones, and your patients or clients through your observations and your ability to work with the malleable aspects of the face.

I hope that the topics in this book suggest the richness of morphology and the joy and great usefulness you can find here. However, to reiterate, although many things said here can be connotative, morphology is a denotative art, and there are many balancing features in one's face to compensate for what may be considered a weakness or flaw. So please, when looking at yourself or others, remember the compassionate aspect of face morphology and be honorable, as this is a sacred art and it is never to be used to gain power over another.

To all health practitioners of every discipline, it is my sincere hope and prayer that this compendium aids and assists you in the diagnosis and assessment of your patients and enhances your relationship with them. May the revelations you receive from this understanding of morphology further your movement toward health, light, love, and self-awareness.

To educators of all varieties, especially the teachers of our young ones, I hope that by reading this book you will understand the individuality of each of your students. It is my intention that this understanding will help you transmit in a compassionate and loving way the knowledge and experiences you wish for them to learn.

It is also my hope that teachers will understand that the learning styles of individuals are different and will see how morphology can reveal that. For instance, so many children are now labeled with ADD and ADHD, and while these labels may apply, it may also be that they are Sanguine types who need to be motoric and learn while they are moving. On the other hand, the highly intellective Nervous types may have the ability to understand deep concepts and teachings, but they need frequent breaks. While the Bilious do not need frequent breaks and have a great capacity to absorb information, they have difficulty dealing with authority and so might resist instruction for this reason. Lymphatic types do not mind sitting in a chair for hours on end and absorbing all the information. They make teachers very happy. While these are generalizations, and every individual is unique, I believe these guideposts can help teachers to understand their students and achieve the result they want, which is for their students to learn.

To all parents, caregivers, guardians, and family members learning this system, it is also my prayer that as your understanding of what is in the pages of this book deepens, a new awareness will awaken in you. As you develop your skills, you may be better able to notice any changes in the face—whether they be of physiological, mental, or emotional significance—that can occur in you, your family members, and your loved ones. Through these new insights you are empowered to support your own healing and the healing of those you love.

And perhaps closest to my heart is that through this understanding we can all learn to appreciate and celebrate our differences as unique expressions of each of our paths in life.

It has been my honor and privilege to be in the lineage of this work. Dr. Gerald Epstein presented the body of knowledge that allowed this book to come into being and offered his genius in a generous gift that I have had the privilege of presenting to you. I thank all of you for reading this book and wish you all the joys and revelations morphology has to offer. It has brought great value to me, my patients, and all others that have shared in its rich, forty-five-hundred-year-old history.

Face Morphology Reference Tables

I have included quick-glance tables here that reveal many of the first-sight observations you may have when you look at the face and get that intuitive hit. The first table is a correlation between facial part and organ/system, while the second table is related to psychological or emotional traits and how they show up on the face. Just a reminder: While these tables are here for you to be able to reference quickly, they are not here to enable you to make a judgment about any individual. When you look at a face and a certain characteristic jumps out at you, and your curiosity says, "I wish I knew what that meant," this table is here to guide you. Please note that when more than one trait is listed, one of the meanings may be more pertinent than the other, depending on the configuration of the face.

This forty-five-hundred-year-old oral tradition has been passed from teacher to student. I can share with you as far back as knowing that Madame Colette Aboulker-Muscat's father taught her, she taught Dr. Gerald Epstein, and he taught me. In my studies with Dr. Epstein there were at times input from other students of Madame Colette. The following tables are credited to the flow of this wisdom through this ancient lineage.

CORRELATION BETWEEN FACIAL PART AND ORGAN/SYSTEM

Facial Part	Organ/System
Lower outer edge of eye (also known as breast mount or mount prominence)	Breast
Hollow between lower outer edge of eye and the prominent part of the cheek	Umbilicus
Median part of nose	Respiratory system
Nose tip	Heart
Prominence situated in front of ears	Hip
Prominent part of cheek	Upper abdomen, stomach
Medial cheek	Lung
Cheekbones	Thorax
Prominence on lower part of cheek	Thigh
Upper lip	Sexual organs, prostate
Lower lip	Kidney, bladder, skin, large intestine, intestinal tract
Mount behind jaw	Knees
Mount in middle of jaw	Calf

FORMS OF THE FACE AND PSYCHOLOGICAL TRAIT

Forms of the Face	Psychological or Emotional Trait
FOREHEAD	
Straight forehead	Homebody
Smooth forehead	Outlook toward future
Very high forehead	Mysticism
Very wide forehead	Thinker
Low set forehead/eye	Realism, practicality
Prominent upper forehead	Idealism
Prominent middle forehead	Deluded, dreamer

Forms of the Face	Psychological or Emotional Trait
FOREHEAD *(continued)*	
Prominent lower forehead	Courage
Prominence on side of forehead	Strong reasoning ability
Forehead bulging in middle	Intellectual pride
Depression in middle of forehead	Lack of self-confidence
Long central vertical line, vein, or hollow in middle of forehead	Need for action, desire for adventure
Horizontal line or crease on forehead	Feelings of inferiority, irregular concentration
Receding lower forehead	Ability to perceive
Hair projecting on forehead	Low intelligence
EAR	
Well-formed ear	Happy associations
Misshapen ears	Grumpiness
Small ears	Insecurity
Big ears	Stable job, stable home
Narrow ear	Nervousness/touchiness
Ears stuck to skull (ears lie flat)	Courtesy, smartness, being dependent
Flaring ears detached from the head	Independence
Floppy ears	Vulgarity
No earlobe or earlobe glued to cranium	Influenced by opposite sex, excellent with money
Large lobe of the ears	Indifference to opposite sex
Turned earlobe	Disrespect for opposite sex
Frontal wrinkles of ear lobe	Sexual vulgarity
EYES	
Bright clear eyes	Vitality
Big open eyes	Strong need for affection

Forms of the Face	Psychological or Emotional Trait
EYES *(continued)*	
Round eyes	Ignorance and naïveté, fear of the future
Bulging eyes	Lovestruck countenance
Eyes set back	Unfaithfulness
Eyes set low (pulled down or slanted downward)	Malice, cheating
Depression at corner of eye	Awkwardness
Dark and hollow under eye	Excessive nervousness
Long eyelashes (upper lid)	Affective sensitivity, increased emotionality
Upper eyelid makes a pocket, or lax/droopy upper lid	Excessive emotion, abnormal affective interactions
EYEBROWS	
Lack of eyebrows (sparse)	Sluggishness
Thick eyebrows	Rigidity/stiffness
Joined eyebrows	Slow to process and integrate information
Eyebrow close to eyes	Aware concentration
Eyebrows far from eyes	Distractibility
Drooping eyebrows	Unpleasant relationships
Center eyebrow convex	Doubtfulness
Winged eyebrows	Irresponsibility
Beginning of eyebrow descending or straight	Lack of trust, suspicion, skepticism
NOSE	
Short nose	Fun-loving and joyful disposition
Long nose	Trustworthiness, continuity and persistence, loves routine, good teacher

Forms of the Face	Psychological or Emotional Trait
NOSE *(continued)*	
Long nose, pulled down nostrils	Patience
Narrow nose	Fear of physical pain
Nose crooked in middle	Lack of honor
Nose projected up	Strong impulses
Protruding nose	Explosiveness
Convex nose	Sense of organization
Concave nose	Devotion
Convex or low bridge of the nose	Financial interest
High nose bridge	Complicated philosophy
Hollow nose bridge	Search for pleasure, possible irresponsibility
Too narrow nose bridge	Paralysis
Wide nose bridge	Physical courage, powerful decisions, philosophical, powerful
Very wide nose bridge	Occultism
Extremely wide nose bridge	Mental unsteadiness
Extremity of nose wide	Explosive mood, general vulgarity
Flaring of nostrils	Impatience
Prominence on side of nostril	Conscious alertness
Cleft on tip of nose	Indecision
CHEEK	
Full cheeks	Strong energy
Hollow cheeks	Courage, alertness, daring, retaliation
Wide cheeks	Need for rest
Big and wide cheeks	Fear of new things and consequences
High cheekbones	Desire for paternity

Forms of the Face	Psychological or Emotional Trait
CHEEK *(continued)*	
Dimple on cheek	Childishness and immaturity
Oblique crease on cheek	Unconscious alertness
MOUTH	
Small mouth	Need for loveliness
Big mouth	Need for social contact
Weak mouth	Artistic talent
Weak mouth, retracted lower lip	Sweet disposition
Flat mouth	Arrogance/braggadocio, bluffer
Mouth slanted inward	Geniality
Sucked-in mouth	Self-satisfaction
Protruding mouth	Ambition
Upward-tilting corners of mouth	Optimism
Droopy mouth corners	Pessimism
Wrinkle at corner of mouth	Opposition
LIPS	
Thin lips	Intransigence
Wide lips	Gusto for life
Epicurean lips	Gusto for taste
Full lips	Generosity
Fleshy lips	Love of earthly pleasures
Pulled-in upper lip	Sexual self-control
Pointing upper lip	Sensitivity
Protruding upper lip	High sexual desire
Fleshy corner of upper lip	Sexual brutality
Lip loose in center	Gift for speech
Fleshy lower lip	Physical pleasures

Forms of the Face	Psychological or Emotional Trait
LIPS *(continued)*	
Firm/muscular lower lip	Authority, ability to defend oneself
Weak mouth, retracted lower lip	Sweet disposition, pleasantness
Forward lower lip	Sassiness, back talk
Protruding lower lip	Aggressiveness, hostility, combativeness
Point under lower lip	Shyness
Vertical lines on lips	Avoidance of social life
CHIN	
Short chin	Quick determination
Long chin	Facile with language
Pointed chin	Impulsive determination
Forward chin	Strong determination, search for fame, glory, and honor
Chin round and fleshy	Suggestibility
Fleshy chin	Need for security
Double/triple chin	Excessive need for comfort and food
Cleft chin	Fickleness and moodiness
Horizontal line across mentalis muscle of chin	Doubtfulness
JAW	
Straight jaw	Powerful stability
Wide strong jaw	Excessive stability
Fleshy jaw	Taste for wealth
Jaw short in back	Mobility
Jaw wide in back	Stubbornness
Oblique line of jaw	Limberness

Forms of the Face	Psychological or Emotional Trait
MISCELLANEOUS	
Delicate skin	Strong sensitivity
Short face	Joyfulness, quickness
Long face	Slowness
Narrow/acute facial angle	Ingeniousness, sleekness and craftiness, shrewdness, malevolence
Wide face	Less sexual refinement
Forward face	Dynamic
Angular face	Difficult disposition
Harmonious face	Pleasant good nature
Small facial openings	Introversion
Wide facial openings	Extroversion
Widow's peak	Seductiveness, charming to opposite sex
No space between front teeth	Respect for authority
Large space between front teeth	No respect for authority
COMBINATIONS	
Wrinkles between eyebrow and lid of eye	Moral dissipation
Eye turned inward, tented nostrils	Jealousy, envy
Small ears/big cheeks	Needs much sleep
Strong back of jaw, wrinkle on upper forehead, straight center eyebrow	Headstrong, stubborn
Large mouth, dimple on chin	Needs companionship
Square chin, eyes stare inward	Egotism
Little flesh on chin, small ears	Drifter

Bibliography

Encausse, Gérard Anaclet Vincent (a.k.a. Papus). *Les Artes Divinatoires.* 1895.

Epstein, Gerald. *Healing Visualizations: Creating Health through Imagery.* New York: Bantam, 1989.

Gaussin, Jean. *Connaitre les autres par: le visage.* Paris: La Bibliotheque du CEPL, 1973.

Hauck, Dennis William. *Sorcerer's Stone: A Beginner's Guide to Alchemy.* New York: Citadel Press Kensington Publishing Corp., 2004.

Trismegistus, Hermes. *The Corpus Hermeticum.* Translated by G. R. S. Mead. Charlotte, N.C.: Information Age Publishing, 2009.

Index